To Dick Smart, an inspiration in fighting the good fight.

~ PREFACE ~

I've been thinking recently about "itching ears" (see 10 December). The Apostle Paul, in his last letter, warns Timothy:

> "The time will come when men will not endure sound doctrine; but after their own lusts shall they heap to themselves teachers, having itching ears; And they shall turn away their ears from the truth, and shall be turned unto fables." (2 Timothy 4:3-4)

Itches demand to be scratched. And fools demand fables. That's the natural state of us all. By nature we say to God what the Israelites said to Isaiah:

> "Prophesy not unto us right things, speak unto us smooth things, prophesy deceits." (Isaiah 30:10)

We must face this about ourselves. As we awake, there will be a large part of us that craves pleasant lies. And there will be any number of false prophets to feed them to us. But such lies bind and blind – they enslave and they darken our understanding.

We need, what my friend Paul calls, a 'Daily Dose of Doctrine.' We need the truth from outside us to challenge and comfort us. This is what the Apostle commands:

> Continue thou in the things which thou hast learned and hast been assured of, knowing of whom thou hast learned them; And that from a child thou hast known the holy scriptures, which are able to make thee wise unto salvation through faith which is in Christ Jesus. (2 Timothy 3:14-15)

Here is the remedy for itching ears. "Continue" in the certain knowledge of the Holy Scriptures. "Continue" might have been translated "abide" or "remain". It's the sense of *making our home* in the Scriptures. Lies and fables are knocking at the door. We make our home in the word.

Why? In order to be Biblio-philes? No, in order to be Christo-philes. The purpose of the Scriptures is to "make us wise unto salvation through faith which is in Christ Jesus." In *Him* is salvation and the Scriptures present Him to us again and again. Through poetry and prophecy, history and allegory, letters and lyrics, Christ is offered to us.

I pray that you will get your Daily Dose of Doctrine and I pray that, through it, you will meet with the LORD Jesus. May He not merely scratch your itch. May He feed your soul, may He make you wise, may He give you life again.

> "Give us this day our daily bread." (Matthew 6:11)

Out of the mouths of babes

We might think of today's phrase as an ancient equivalent of "Kids say the darnedest things." But Jesus was making a deeper point. He wasn't just pointing us to children. He was encouraging us to child-like-ness. It is not only infants, but more generally the simple *trusters* in Jesus whose surprising wisdom will shock the world.

To understand this teaching we need to know that Jesus splits the world into the "wise" and the "babes."

> "I thank thee, O Father, Lord of heaven and earth, because thou hast hid these things from the wise and prudent, and hast revealed them unto babes." (Matthew 11:25)

The wise and prudent are self-reliant and self-assured. They don't need Jesus and they don't want Him. The "babes" are dependent and happy to be so. They know their desperate need and are not ashamed to *receive* from the Lord of life.

An eight year old could play the part of the wise and prudent. And an eighty year old could be one of the "babes." It's not about age but about guileless dependence.

How does Jesus react to these two groups?

Well previously we saw Jesus "cleansing the temple." The religious had turned His house of prayer into a den of thieves. He violently opposes their religious posturing, overturning the tables.

You might think that such aggression would frighten the little ones. We could imagine that the timid and weak would be disturbed and stay at a distance. In fact, the opposite is true. When they see Him overturn the tables of the *strong*, the weak are magnetically drawn to Him:

> "And the blind and the lame came to him in the temple; and he healed them. And when the chief priests and scribes saw the wonderful things that he did, and the children crying in the temple, and saying, Hosanna to the Son of David; they were sore displeased, And said unto him, Hearest thou what these say? And Jesus saith unto them, Yea; have ye never read, Out of the mouth of babes and sucklings thou hast perfected praise?"
> (Matthew 21:14-16)

The blind, the lame and the children are not put off by Christ's strength because they see it employed in their liberation. The very weakest members of society flock to this holy Rioter, perhaps still holding His whip!

What kind of personality can walk into the holiest place on earth, throw around the furniture and so attract the wrath of the authorities *and* the love of the little ones? In this world, there are some who can face down the powers that be. And there are some who can win the trust and affection of the weak and timid. But Jesus does both. He stands between the "wise" and the "babes", giving both exactly what they need. In the process He polarizes them even further!

And *then* He quotes Scripture. He's not some outlaw with the support of a rebellious fringe. He is the ultimate Law Abiding Citizen (Galatians 4:4). He doesn't stand on one side against the other – He comes from above with the wisdom of heaven. And so He gives them the biblical explanation for it all:

> "Out of the mouth of babes and sucklings hast thou ordained strength because of thine enemies, that thou mightest still the enemy and the avenger." (Psalm 8:2)

The children had been applying the Messianic title: "Son of David" to Jesus. The authorities want Him to disown it. But Jesus says, No, remember the Psalm, you need to *listen* to the "babes."

In the world of Psalm 8, Jesus is the Son of Man/Son of David, the little children are the "babes" and the chief priests and scribes… who are the? They are the "enemies"! Yet, here's a wonderful thought. How is the battle between the "Son of David" and His enemies to be adjudicated? By the little children.

What "stills" the enemy? Not just a bigger whip. What stills the enemy is the praise of the little ones. You see the Son of David is not vindicated by the size of His army, but by the simple-hearted praise of the "babes."

I speak to many Christians who worry about their feebleness in witness. They lament that they don't give impressive proofs to their friends and family regarding Jesus. But Jesus is not the kind of Lord who is vindicated by worldly strength. He is vindicated by the blind, the lame and the infants. The words that best point to Christ are the words "out of the mouths of babes." Because "wisdom is justified by her *children*." (Matthew 11:19)

Render unto Caesar the things that are Caesar's

In chess terms they call it a "fork". Your opponent puts you in a position where, whatever you do, you will lose a piece. The Pharisees and Herodians (*not* a natural alliance) gang up on Jesus "to catch Him in His words." (Mark 12:13)

> "They say unto him, Master, we know that thou art true, and carest for no man: for thou regardest not the person of men, but teachest the way of God in truth: Is it lawful to give tribute to Caesar, or not? Shall we give, or shall we not give?" (Mark 12:14-15)

If Jesus says "give", He loses His Jewish support. If He says "don't give", the Romans will shut Him up before the words leave His lips.

And, 2000 years later, we face a similar quandary. If Jesus says "give" doesn't that mean His disciples lose their distinctiveness in the world? Perhaps we're just meant to blend into the political landscape and stand for nothing.

Alternatively if He says "don't give", we might be consigned to a perpetual contrarian position as regards politics. Christians would then, by definition, become terrible citizens in the world's eyes.

So which is it to be? Well Jesus has already shown His brilliance at escaping such traps. And here we are treated to another famous riposte:

> "But [Jesus], knowing their hypocrisy, said unto them, Why tempt ye me? bring me a penny, that I may see it. And they brought it. And he saith unto them, Whose is this image and superscription? And they said unto him, Caesar's. And Jesus answering said unto them, **Render to Caesar the things that are Caesar's, and to God the things that are God's**. And they marvelled at him." (Mark 12:15-17)

Notice that Jesus has to borrow a coin to make His point. Here is a Man who had nowhere to lay His head (Matthew 8:20). He rode into town on a borrowed donkey (Matthew 21:2), He was laid in a borrowed tomb (Matthew 27:60) and when He died, they gambled for His only possessions, His garments (Matthew 27:35). When it comes to money, Jesus speaks with complete integrity. He's not in love with money, as the Pharisees were (Luke 16:14). We can trust what He says here because we know it is not motivated by the least degree of *self*-interest.

And when He gets His hands on a coin, notice what He brings to our attention… the image. That is the key to this teaching. We give to Caesar what is Caesar's ***image***. The image-bearer *belongs* to the original.

Do the Pharisees agree to this? If so they walk into a trap of Jesus' own making…

We must give to God what is *God's image*. And what is God's image? We are! (Genesis 1:26ff)

Here the tables are turned on Christ's questioners. *Both* the Jews *and* the Romans are challenged on the most fundamental level. It's not about the paying of taxes. It's not about the recognition or legitimacy of state power. It's about whether we belong to God!

And if we do, then there will always be ways of honouring the temporal authority of the state – even if sometimes it takes a miracle to do so (Matthew 17:24-27).

The Pharisees might have considered civic disobedience to be the height of holy living. Jesus says, You've missed the point. Do you belong to God? That is the question.

> "Render to Caesar the things that are Caesar's, and to God the things that are God's."

3 October – Matthew 23:1-12

They do not practise what they preach

— *The adulterous pastor who campaigns for "family values."*

— *The drug-taking sports star portraying a spotless image to sponsors.*

— *The socialist MP who sends her children to exclusive prep-schools.*

The world despises leaders who don't practise what they preach. And so does Jesus. In fact Jesus leads the way in the condemnation:

> "Then spake Jesus to the multitude, and to his disciples, Saying The scribes and the Pharisees sit in Moses' seat: All therefore whatsoever they bid you observe, that observe and do; but do not ye after their works: for they say, and do not. For they bind heavy burdens and grievous to be borne, and lay them on men's shoulders; but they themselves will not move them with one of their fingers. But all their works they do for to be seen of men: they make broad their phylacteries, and enlarge the borders of

> their garments, And love the uppermost rooms at feasts, and the chief seats in the synagogues, And greetings in the markets, and to be called of men, Rabbi, Rabbi." (Matthew 23:1-7)

These words from Christ would have fallen like asteroids onto the cultural and religious scene of His day. Jesus is opening fire on the holiest people these Jews had ever seen! The scribes and Pharisees were the best of the best. The greatest Bible scholars, the strictest moral leaders. It was *the scribes and Pharisees* who chastised the culture from the vantage point of the religious right. But somehow Jesus outflanks them. Not so much from the right, but *from above.* The assembled crowd would have been astounded. And the scribes and Pharisees would be choking with righteous indignation.

But in Matthew chapter 23, Jesus delivers the sharpest volley of criticism seen anywhere in the Gospels. And who is on the receiving end? The publicans? The Samaritans? The Romans? The sinners? No. The *religious*!

Here is the Prophet *par excellence* doing what prophets do best: uncovering the pretensions of religious leaders. It is public. It is sharp-tongued. It is brutal. And it is unrelenting.

How does Jesus come by such a clear vision of His target? How is He able to see through the religious window-dressing? Is it simply because He is the Son of God and therefore "knows what is in a man?" (John 2:25). Well there is that. But if we let Him, Jesus will train *us* in how to see our leaders.

These verses tell us three things:

1. Jesus was not fooled by what they say.

   In modern translations it says "they do not practice what they preach." This is the mark of an authentic teacher – their life is open to scrutiny and free from hypocrisy. The Pharisees failed the test.

2. Jesus was not fooled by what they did "to be seen by men."

   The evolutionary psychologists will tell us of a thousand motivations towards "goodness" all of which are ultimately selfish. There is a "goodness" that springs only from pride and it is odious in Christ's sight.

3. Jesus recognised their selfishness in giving burdens but refusing to take them.

   There is such poetic imagery here: "they bind heavy burdens and grievous to be borne, and lay them on men's shoulders; but they themselves will not move them with one of their fingers." They 'lay down the law' but never bear one another up! This is a clear sign that they are not authentic ministers of God's word. And Jesus blasts them with a truly righteous indignation.

But what about Jesus Himself? When He preaches "practice what you preach" does He practice *this* preaching?

Well let's consider number 1. Here is a Preacher who commands "Love your enemies, bless them that curse you, do good to them that hate you, and pray for them which despitefully use you, and persecute you." (Matthew 5:44) And as He is killed by His enemies, He prays "Father, forgive them; for they know not what they do." (Luke 23:34)

What about number 2? Think of the Mount of Olives the night before He died. It was an ancient escape route from Jerusalem in times of trouble (2 Samuel 15). There is Jesus on top of the mountain, the mob has not yet come to arrest Him and His disciples are asleep. If ever there was a time to run, this was it. Yet, when the eyes of all men were shut, Jesus remained and prayed and accepted the cup of suffering from His Father's hand.

What about number 3? Christ came not to weigh us down but to lift us up. He is the true Preacher of God's Word because ultimately He does *not* burden His people but carry them.

> "Come unto me, all ye that labour and are heavy laden, and I will give you rest." (Matthew 11:28)

4 October – Matthew 23:13-26

The blind leading the blind

Three times Jesus uses this image in the Gospels:

> "Can the blind lead the blind? shall they not both fall into the ditch?" (Luke 6:39)
>
> "They be blind leaders of the blind. And if the blind lead the blind, both shall fall into the ditch." (Matthew 15:14)
>
> "Woe unto you, ye blind guides." (Matthew 23:16)

When we use the saying we usually lament the ignorance of the leader, or perhaps their naivety. Essentially the leader doesn't *know* enough. That's what puts them in the dark and makes them an incompetent leader.

But the way Jesus uses the phrase is different. He consistently applies the phrase to the Pharisees. And it's not their lack of knowledge that is the problem. Their problem is their hypocrisy. It's the fact that they don't practise what they preach that blinds them.

We have already seen how hypocrisy is like a beam in our eye while we berate our brother for the speck in his. While-ever we are pointing the finger at others and ignoring the sinfulness of our own hearts we remain blind.

This is a frightening truth. We tend to think that we have a pretty good grip on reality. We imagine that, whatever other problems we might have, we can at least see the world for what it is. But Jesus says that clear vision is not at all common. Our eyes are not wide open, not naturally.

Why not? We are inveterate self-justifiers. We are committed to a view of ourselves that then shapes our view of everything else. If we invest in a pious identity then something will have to give. Because we are *not* pious. We are sinners. Yet, in order to square the circle of our sin on the one hand and our need to project a "righteous" image on the other, we will have to deal in unrealities. We will have to lie. We will have to recalibrate and justify and mask and ignore and exaggerate and over-compensate. And such a re-adjustment of the truth comes at a heavy cost. We lose our ability to see! We lose touch with reality. And if the *leaders* are out of touch with reality, God help those who are being led.

The Office is a study in how not to lead. David Brent (or, in America, Michael Scott) proves to be the worst boss imaginable largely because of his own need to be vindicated. The office must revolve around his ego and everyone suffers.

If you are in leadership of some kind you will want to lead well. You won't want to be a blind guide. Yet the clear vision which Jesus urges upon us is not, first and foremost, about increasing our skills and knowledge base. Ultimately it's about losing our hypocrisy. Drop the mask, and the blinders come off.

We need to see *ourselves* clearly as those who naturally *belong* in the pit. And yet Christ has entered in and lifted us to the throne. We are helpless, filthy, unworthy but blessed beyond measure.

Now, as we confess our sin and receive Christ's alien righteousness we give up on the wearisome burdens of our own self-justification. Now we realise that life is not about *us* and our own little holiness project. Now we are freed to lead, which, in Christ's book, means to serve. And perhaps then we will lead others away from the pit.

Strain at a gnat and swallow a camel

> "There was an old lady who swallowed a cow, to catch the dog, to catch the cat, to catch the bird, to catch the spider, that wriggled and wiggled and tickled inside her. She swallowed the spider to catch the fly. I don't know why she swallowed the fly – Perhaps she'll die!" (Traditional Nursery Rhyme)

Children love this daft imagery and sing along with glee. No-one thinks that there is a class of "old lady" who are being "got at" with the nursery rhyme. No-one could be as stupid as this "old lady", surely!

Yet the picture Jesus paints is equally absurd. Jesus thinks that there *are* people who fit the mould. What's even more shocking is that they are the most straight-laced, respectable people in society. But Jesus describes them as plain ridiculous.

So what does He do? He ridicules them. Relentlessly. That is the whole point of Matthew 23.

The mind has been compared more closely to a portrait gallery than a debating chamber. Certainly Jesus is a master of the striking image. He paints evocative verbal pictures that linger long in the imagination. Just consider how He exposes the hypocrisy of the Pharisees in this chapter:

> "Woe unto you, scribes and Pharisees, hypocrites! for ye devour widows' houses, and for a pretence make long prayer: therefore ye shall receive the greater damnation. Woe unto you, scribes and Pharisees, hypocrites! for ye compass sea and land to make one proselyte, and when he is made, ye make him twofold more the child of hell than yourselves. Woe unto you, ye blind guides, which say, Whosoever shall swear by the temple, it is nothing; but whosoever shall swear by the gold of the temple, he is a debtor! Ye fools and blind: for whether is greater, the gold, or the temple that sanctifieth the gold? And, Whosoever shall swear by the altar, it is nothing; but whosoever sweareth by the gift that is upon it, he is guilty. Ye fools and blind: for whether is greater, the gift, or the altar that sanctifieth the gift? Whoso therefore shall swear by the altar, sweareth by it, and by all things thereon. And whoso shall swear by the temple, sweareth by it, and by him that dwelleth therein. And he that shall swear by heaven, sweareth by the throne of God, and by him that sitteth thereon. Woe unto you, scribes and Pharisees, hypocrites! for ye pay tithe

> of mint and anise and cummin, and have omitted the weightier matters of the law, judgment, mercy, and faith: these ought ye to have done, and not to leave the other undone."
> (Matthew 23:14-23)

This catalogue of double-standards is shocking:

By day they defraud widows of their property, by night they lead prayer meetings.

They debate the minutiae of temple oaths while spreading the kingdom of Satan.

They take pride in tithing from their window box yet care nothing about the beating heart of the law: justice, mercy and faith.

That's the evidence which stands against them. So how will Jesus, the Prosecutor, sum up? Will He accuse them of committing some logical fallacy, using impressive Latin labels? Will He produce a report with strongly worded findings? No, He makes fun of them:

> "Ye blind guides, which **strain at a gnat, and swallow a camel**." (Matthew 23:14)

We have already discussed the absurdity of the blind leading the blind. In the same breath Jesus comes up with another even more absurd mental picture. He asks us to imagine a fastidious diner fussing over the tiniest insect, all the while oblivious to the hulking great dromedary he's gulping down.

If there is a "Waiter, Waiter" joke as ridiculous as this one, I haven't heard it.

> *Waiter, waiter, there's a fly in my soup.*
>
> *Allow me to fish that out for you sir. You wouldn't want to spoil your appetite for the hippo.*

This phrase is more than an absurd verbal picture. It's also a play on words. In Aramaic, Jesus' mother tongue, gnat is *gamla* and camel is *gamal.* So essentially these Pharisees can't sort out their *gamlas* from their *gamals.* And the results are disastrous.

The religious leaders show an appalling lack of proportion. They're like Emergency Room doctors who refuse to treat a dying patient because of a technicality. Peripheral matters blind them to the bleeding obvious. How did they become so ridiculous?

Answer: By doing exactly what we're tempted to do every day. More on that tomorrow …

Whited sepulchre

Last time we considered the absurd lack of proportion demonstrated by the Pharisees. They strained at gnats and swallowed camels. In other words, they obsessed over minutiae and ignored the whole point of the Scriptures.

How did it come to this? How did they end up having such a diabolical problem with perspective?

The answer is that they made the kinds of errors that we are tempted to make every day. They focused on externals, whilst ignoring the festering darkness within.

> "Woe unto you, scribes and Pharisees, hypocrites! for ye make clean the outside of the cup and of the platter, but within they are full of extortion and excess. Thou blind Pharisee, cleanse first that which is within the cup and platter, that the outside of them may be clean also. Woe unto you, scribes and Pharisees, hypocrites! for ye are like unto **whited sepulchres**, which indeed appear beautiful outward, but are within full of dead men's bones, and of all uncleanness. Even so ye also outwardly appear righteous unto men, but within ye are full of hypocrisy and iniquity." (Matthew 23:25-28)

On the outside there is cleanliness, brilliant white, beauty and apparent righteousness.

On the inside there is extortion, excess, death, uncleanness, hypocrisy and iniquity.

And the stand-out image to encapsulate this split-personality is a "whited sepulchre." Tyndale translated it "paynted tombes." Coverdale has "paynted sepulcres" The Geneva Bible says "whited tombes." More modern translations say "white-washed tombs." It's a compelling picture. Imagine it, freshly painted, gleaming in the Mediterranean sun. Dazzling on the outside. Death on the inside. And that's not simply a picture of an institution. Jesus is speaking of *people.* These *people* were white-washed tombs.

Here is the reason for their imbalance between 'the weightier matters of the law', and the trivia with which they concerned themselves: there was a deeper imbalance between their internal and their external world. They were so concerned to appear brilliant that all their efforts were thrown into "operation white-wash." Hidden acts of kindness were useless. Ostentation and boasting were the order of the day. It was a "Get pious quick" scheme and it left them spiritually bankrupt. They only did what would exalt themselves in the eyes of others – and bringing a tithe of their garden herbs to the temple was perfect for this low-cost, high-impact publicity drive. The weightier matters of justice, mercy and faith – they were too long-term, too labour-intensive, too hidden! And so their righteousness was as thin as a coat of paint. Underneath it was uncleanness and iniquity.

Does any of this hit home with us? Are we drawn towards the "Get pious quick" schemes? What do we make into our own barometers of spiritual health? Do we settle for a trivial externalism? Do we measure ourselves against mere box-ticking Christianity? Are our eyes on the rituals that keep up appearances while the "inside of the cup" is anything but clean?

Well if we've been following Jesus' teaching we ought to know that *everyone* has a problem with the "inside of the cup."

> "Out of the heart proceed evil thoughts, murders, adulteries, fornications, thefts, false witness, blasphemies: These are the things which defile a man." (Matthew 15:19-20)

So if we've all got this problem, how do we "clean the inside of the cup"? Is it about turning our gaze firmly towards our navel? Is the answer a re-doubling of our private spiritual disciplines?

Well there are a number of problems with that as a solution. Firstly, the internally focused Christian will end up being just as neglectful of 'the weightier matters' of justice and mercy as the religious exhibitionist. The focus may have switched from external to internal, but what is really required is a decisive shift from self to neighbour. And that shift has to come from elsewhere.

The second problem with trying to "clean the inside of the cup" *ourselves* is the sheer magnitude of the task. Stemming the flow of "evil thoughts, murders, adulteries, etc" with personal piety is like trying to dam Niagara Falls with a cork. There's only one clean-up operation sufficient for the task. The prophet Ezekiel speaks of it in chapter 36:

> "Then will I sprinkle clean water upon you, and ye shall be clean: from all your filthiness, and from all your idols, will I cleanse you. A new heart also will I give you, and a new spirit will I put within you: and I will take away the stony heart out of your flesh, and I will give you an heart of flesh. And I will put my spirit within you, and cause you to walk in my statutes, and ye shall keep my judgments, and do them. And ye shall dwell in the land that I gave to your fathers; and ye shall be my people, and I will be your

> God. I will also save you from all your uncleannesses." (Ezekiel 36:25-29)

Here is a heavenly heart transplant which only the LORD Jesus can offer. But if we have it, our world is turned inside-out! Now that we've been cleansed, we can forget about "operation white-wash". The eyes of heaven see us as clean, the eyes of the world are just not that important. We dazzle in our Father's eyes, we don't need to outshine our neighbours. No, now we can love our neighbours. And it has nothing to do with our own little holiness project. It has nothing to do with climbing the rankings of our spiritual communities. We are released from the need to justify ourselves and suddenly we can serve.

Not a white-washed tomb. Christians have put down the paint brush. We are those who admit to our filth and spiritual deadness. But we are those who have been saved from our uncleannesses. Now we have nothing to prove. Nothing to lose. Nothing to hide. Now we can love. And such love is the fulfilling of the law.

7 October – Matthew 23:37-39

I would have gathered thy children as a hen gathereth her chickens

Jesus calls the Pharisees a lot of names in Matthew chapter 23. They are hypocrites – not practicing what they preach. They are blind guides. They are absurdly imbalanced moralists – 'straining at a gnat and swallowing a camel'. They are whited sepulchers, they are serpents, vipers and murderers, the very apex of evil in the history of God's people (v33-36).

Yet what does He call them at the end? Children. Chicks even.

> "O Jerusalem, Jerusalem, thou that killest the prophets, and stonest them which are sent unto thee, **how often would I have gathered thy children together, even as a hen gathereth her chickens under her wings**, and ye would not!" (Matthew 23:37)

Notice first who Jesus claims to be in this verse. He is the One who has sent prophets to Jerusalem over the centuries. He is the One always longing to gather Israel. He is the One who feels an ancient, parental love for the people of God.

Jesus weeps over Jerusalem (Luke 19:41) because He has always wept over Jerusalem. Now He stands in its midst, an unschooled Rabbi, seemingly a 'minority of one' taking on the religious establishment. Yet notice the towering "I" He unleashes in this teaching: "How often would ***I*** have gathered thy children." Jesus considers Himself the driving force of Israel's history. Here is the Lord God among us, and what is He like?

He is like a mother hen. It's an incredible change of tone in verse 37. We have had 36 verses of blistering condemnation. Yet in none of those verses does Jesus mention His divine identity. Those assessments might have been made by any religious observer with eyes to see it. The Pharisees themselves would have considered it a critique from below. But now Jesus invokes His ancient authority as Lord of Israel. In verse 37 He draws Himself up to His true height, and when He does so, how does He appear to the people? As a hen gathering chicks.

This is the true heart of Zion's King. He has intense motherly concern for these snakes, these killers, these white-washed tombs. He longs to gather them. Whatever we have said about the warrant for harsh words and ridicule in this chapter we must recognize that the last word is grace. Jesus is not "writing off" these wicked men, He's pursuing them. And the pointing of His finger serves the welcome of His wings. This should also be our heart if ever we offer stinging rebuke. The point is not to crush but to gather.

But these Pharisees will have none of it. And so the *real* condemnation of the self-righteous is not so much their resistance to the rebukes as their refusal of the relationship. It is grace that constitutes them as sinners – the offer of mercy which occasions their reprobation.

Our discussions about God's love and God's anger can become very abstract. This verse makes it personal. The love of God has shown up among us and His name is Jesus. He is the eternal Gatherer – the One who longs to reconcile a people to the Father. His anger is the response of love to wilful children who refuse His grace.

The Lord God of Israel does not stand behind both love and anger as though He wills one or other according to human worth or some divine caprice. God *is* love and His anger is only ever a response to the thwarting and refusal of this love. He does not become angry in spite of those motherly wings but because of them.

> "Fly sinners, fly into those arms
> Of everlasting love."
>
> — *Charles Wesley, Jesus the Name High Over All*

Wars and rumours of wars

Whatever dominates the skyline of a city tells you what they worship. In that ancient city of Babel, they sought a name for themselves so they tried to build a tower to heaven. In a sense they worshipped themselves. The ancient cities that Paul visited would have been dominated by massive shrines and temples, set up in the high places. Up until the last hundred years, London was dominated by St Paul's Cathedral. Of course today our city skylines continue to be dominated by our objects of worship. Today the great centres of finance tower over us and remind us who we really serve.

In Jesus' day, one building captivated the hearts and minds of the Jews – the temple. And with good reason. In Moses' day the LORD revealed a heavenly blueprint to construct a model of heaven and earth. Moses built this portable model called the tabernacle. And the Glory of the LORD filled the tabernacle with the very Presence of God. Later Solomon built a bigger, solid version of this model of heaven and earth – this was the first temple. Again, the cloud of the LORD's Presence filled this building. Here was the dwelling place of God on earth.

No wonder that the people thought they were safe so long as they had the temple (Jeremiah 7). And no wonder that when the LORD judged the Israelites for their sin He struck at the temple. So in the 6th century BC the Babylonians came and destroyed the temple and carried the people into exile. The people came back after 70 years of exile and built a second temple. This time the temple was desecrated by the Greeks. Then the temple was rebuilt again by 20BC as Herod's Temple. That's the one standing in Jesus' day. And the disciples are *very* impressed by it.

> "And as Jesus went out of the temple, one of his disciples saith unto him, Master, see what manner of stones and what buildings are here!" (Mark 13:1)

Here was the most impressive building a Jew was ever likely to see. Massive stones, magnificent structures. More than this, it's God's house – the place where humans can meet with the Most High. Surely Jesus will also be impressed by the temple. But His reply leaves everyone dumbfounded:

> "And Jesus answering said unto him, Seest thou these great buildings? there shall not be left one stone upon another, that shall not be thrown down." (Mark 13:2)

It's almost impossible to imagine the impression these words would have had on the disciples. Think for a second of those stunned faces witnessing the Twin Towers collapsing – that's the level of shock here. To strike at the heart of America, Al Qaeda struck at the Twin Towers and the Pentagon – symbols of American pride and security. Well, take the shock of that attack and multiply it: because here is God's building – God's house – and Jesus says it will be rubble. He was predicting Jerusalem's destruction in AD70 – but *that* cataclysmic event spoke of an even more cosmic demolition.

After 9/11 America was in a state of shock because if *those* buildings could be struck, nothing was safe. Even more so with the temple. If God's house was going to be demolished then nothing on earth is safe.

After Jesus speaks no-one can say a word. Maybe for an hour. Maybe even longer. In verse 3 we see Jesus sitting on the Mount of Olives, overlooking the temple. No-one can speak as they leave the temple courts, cross the Kidron Valley and climb the Mount of Olives. All are silent because Jesus has spoken of something truly earth-shattering. God's house is going to be demolished. Is nothing safe?

The disturbing answer Jesus gives is 'No'. If God's house is scheduled for demolition, rest assured the rest of the world will follow. That is Mark chapter 13 in a nutshell.

Judgement from heaven always moves from the top down. As 1 Peter 4 declares:

> "Judgment must begin at the house of God." (1 Peter 4:17)

The stones of the temple will be completely broken apart. But that's just the beginnings of things breaking apart.

There will be international breakdown:

> "And when ye shall hear of **wars and rumours of wars**, be ye not trouled: for such things must needs be; but the end shall not be yet. For nation shall rise against nation, and kingdom against kingdom." (Mark 13:7-8)

There will be family breakdown:

> "Now the brother shall betray the brother to death, and the father the son; and children shall rise up against their parents, and shall cause them to be put to death." (Mark 13:12)

Most shockingly, there will be cosmic breakdown:

> "The sun shall be darkened, and the moon shall not give her light, and the stars of heaven shall fall, and the powers that are in heaven shall be shaken." (Mark 13:24-25)

First the temple will be rubble. But one day the whole universe will be rubble.

What hope can there be when, according to Hebrews 12:27, everything that *can* be shaken will be removed? Where will we find security when even the *Temple* resists the saying "safe as houses"? Where can we put our trust when even God's house is scheduled for demolition?

When we hear of "wars and rumours of wars" there's two things we can conclude. Firstly, this age is not a safe time in which to make your home. Secondly, we *are* moving towards a regeneration – through the pains will come new birth. And only the *new* Jerusalem can provide the security we crave.

9 October – Mark 13:1-37

Signs of the times

When "wars and rumours of wars" hit the headlines, Christians will often proclaim, "This must be the end." And often they will point to Mark 13 as proof. Yet in this chapter Jesus says something quite different:

> "And when ye shall hear of wars and rumours of wars, be ye not troubled: for such things must needs be; but *the end shall not be yet.* For nation shall rise against nation, and kingdom against kingdom: and there shall be earthquakes in divers places, and there shall be famines and troubles: these are the beginnings of sorrows." (Mark 13:7-8)

When nations rise against nations, people declare, "These must be the last days." And of course, they are right. Yet "the last days" describe the whole period from Christ's first to His second coming. The last days have been going for 2000 years now.

When we see international breakdown, what should we conclude? Jesus says "These are the beginnings of sorrows." The word for "sorrows" is a word for "birth-pains." Such events might be painful – excruciatingly painful. But they are a pain that leads to new life. These signs are not death-throes but birth-pains. In one sense they represent an ending. But far more they are the ending that births a new beginning.

Back in Matthew 16 Jesus spoke of "**signs of the times**" such as the famous, "red sky at night." (Matthew 16:3,4). These are the kinds of signs Jesus wants us to be attuned to. In Mark 13 He also speaks of the fig tree, whose leaves may be tender now, but such vulnerability signifies a coming summer. Think about these signs. Though the sky is blood red, yet, as we all know "red sky at night, shepherd's *delight*." And though the fig tree is tender now, summer is around the corner.

In just this way Jesus wants us to interpret the signs of family, national, international and cosmic breakdown. They are painful – but painful like pregnancy is painful. There is new life coming.

It would be easy to read Mark 13 merely as a prophecy of doom. But Jesus intends something else beyond these "sorrows."

There is "**the end**" (v7, 13). In Greek it's the word *telos* meaning goal. It is the end for which all things are made. The universe is heading towards its goal.

There is "**birth**" (v8) – the regeneration of all things! (Matthew 19:28)

There is "**summer**" (v27) – after the cold of winter and after the tenderness of the leaves in spring, all creation will blossom. Christ's world will flower and bear fruit.

There is "**the cloud**" (v26) – this is the cloud symbolising the Presence of the LORD with His people (Numbers 10:33-36). Jesus will come with the cloud. It's the cloud that provides shelter by day, light and warmth by night. Jesus will come back in the cloud and neither He nor the cloud of His presence will ever leave us again.

There is "**gathering**" (v27) – as a hen gathers her chicks, Jesus will gather His people. Our lives are scattered in this age, we are distant from one another and from Christ, one day He will gather us.

There is the "**power and glory of Son of Man**" (v26) – The whole cosmos will be shaken, yet one thing will survive. Jesus Himself. Think of how He speaks:

> "Heaven and earth shall pass away: but my words shall not pass away." (Mark 13:31)

It is an astonishing thing to say. Who does He think He is? Well He knows Himself to be the One Person who can last this judgement. He, and in a real sense He alone, is what remains on the other side of this judgement. The last day will be the Day of the LORD.

For He will be the true Temple torn down – the Head of creation taken down to the tomb. Yet from there He will arise. And for those who come *into* Christ, the safe-house, the end will be "summer", "regeneration", "gathering", "the cloud of His presence" and "the power and glory of the Son of Man".

Follow the "signs of the times." This dark night, awash with blood, will give way to a delightful dawn.

10 October – Matthew 25:14-30

Talents

Flourishing economies are hard to come by in world history. Every now and again resources are found, technologies discovered, enemies plundered and wealth increases. But usually it doesn't last very long. This is because, historically, people have only ever known two responses to wealth: we either hoard it or we display it.

We either squirrel it away for a rainy day, (because who knows how long prosperity will last), or we show off our wealth ostentatiously, perhaps building great monuments to ourselves. Of course, in either case the economy stagnates. This is because, whether we hoard or display, we are not re-investing.

But what happens when whole cultures are raised on stories like this one. Read Matthew 25:14-30.

Here the "talents" are not given *for the benefit* of the recipients. They are a trust from the master to the servant. The servant was not to show their talents around town. But nor were the servants to hide their wealth away. They were to put the money to work. And work it did – for those who invested it, that is.

A culture reared on such stories will begin to have a very different attitude to wealth. And so it has proved to be in western civilisation. There has been incredible economic flourishing in cultures where the Bible has held sway, not because its people are more ingenious, and not simply because their resources have been more plentiful. The *attitude* to wealth has been different (we'll consider more on this tomorrow).

But for now let's consider "talents" in the way we have come to understand them (thanks to this parable). What should we do with the abilities that our Lord has given us?

Again the temptations are exactly the same – they travel in one of two directions…

We are tempted to display our gifts in proud ostentation. Most people wouldn't dream of disclosing their bank balance in a conversation, yet we can sprinkle our speech with achievements, connections, claims to fame, anything that would reflect well on us. We flash our talents around like an ancient king looking for adoring subjects. Or…

We hide away – 'keeping our light under a bushel'. Because, here is our fear: If we prove ourselves to be "talented", well, people might expect more from us. Our limits would be tested and our energy depleted. Perhaps it's best, we conclude, just to bury our talents and keep ourselves to ourselves.

Yet Jesus calls us to a third way. We'll see how tomorrow…

11 October – Matthew 25:14-30

Well done, good and faithful servant

We've seen the danger and the opportunity of "talents". Whether it's the monetary unit or the God-given ability, we're tempted to abuse our talents in one of two ways – self-indulgence or cowardly retreat. We either show off our talents in self-promoting ostentation or we bury our talents and keep them from the world. Neither option is Christ's intention. He wants us to be *servants* - using our talents for the blessing of others. But how will we be motivated to move out of our natural responses driven by pride or fear?

The answer from Matthew 25:14-30 is to get a true vision for our Master.

Let's recap the story… one servant is given five talents and makes five more. Another is given two talents and makes two more. The last servant is given one talent and "he went and digged in the earth, and hid his lord's money." (v18) And the reason for his tight-fisted parsimony?

> "Then he which had received the one talent came and said, Lord, I knew thee that thou art an hard man, reaping where thou hast not sown, and gathering where thou hast not strawed: And I was afraid, and went and hid thy talent in the earth: lo, there thou hast that is thine." (Matthew 25:24-25)

This is such a contrast to the way the Lord is portrayed in his dealings with the good servants:

> "**Well done, thou good and faithful servant**: thou hast been faithful over a few things, I will make thee ruler over many things: enter thou into the joy of thy lord." (Matthew 25:21)

The amount which they make their master is not important – whether five talents or two – faithful service of this lord is what counts. After all, both good servants are told that their talents are merely "a few things" when compared to the "many things" he has in store for them. This lord is no grudging miser. He exalts servants to thrones, making them rulers. And not simply rulers, they are intended for the life and love of this lord – entering into his *joy*.

Again let us compare this to the allegations of the third servant. "A hard man, reaping where [he] hast not sown"? An object of dread? One who makes his servants shut down and close off? It is amazing to think that this servant is describing the same lord.

And yet, in response to this meanness, the lord displays exactly the hardness that the servant fears:

> "His lord answered and said unto him, Thou wicked and slothful servant, thou knewest that I reap where I sowed not, and gather where I have not strawed: Thou oughtest therefore to have put my money to the exchangers, and then at my coming I should have received mine own with usury. Take therefore the talent from him, and give it unto him which hath ten talents. For unto every one that hath shall be given, and he shall have abundance: but from him that hath not shall be taken away even that which he hath. And cast ye the unprofitable servant into outer darkness: there shall be weeping and gnashing of teeth."
> (Matthew 25:26-30)

Judgement is repeatedly presented in the Bible as a handing over to the person's mad desires. Everyone gets the lord they trust in. Forever.

Here again we see that the wicked servant gets exactly the kind of lord he looked to. To imagine the Lord of heaven as a harsh task-master will create a certain kind of grudging service, which in turn will result in a certain judgement. On the other hand, trusting a generous Lord to be the One who raises servants to be kings, this produces open-hearted spend-thrifts.

It all turns on how we see the Lord. And how should we see Him? In the next chapter He tears apart bread and says "This is my body". He pours out wine and says "This is my blood." He gives His very *Self* to the world in love and as we look on, how can we not thrill to the invitation "enter into the joy of thy Lord"? It's *that* vision that creates "Good and faithful servants."

12 October – Matthew 25:31-46

The sheep and the goats

The gospel according to Jesus is a little different to the gospel according to me. The gospel according to me tells of a God who is, generally, far off, but when he does involve Himself it mainly concerns me, my loved ones and the success of Australian sports teams. Therefore, when Christ announces His news for the world, I am constantly taken off guard.

In Matthew 25:31-46, Jesus tells the parable of the sheep and the goats. It speaks of the end of history as we know it. Here is a truly earth-shattering event "when the Son of man shall come in his glory and all the holy angels with him." On that day the world will be split in two.

On His right there are the sheep (v33), who are blessed by His Father (v34) and called righteous (v37).

On His left there are the goats (v33), who are cursed and will share in the devil's fate (v41).

The sheep will inherit eternal life, the goats will go to eternal punishment (v46).

And there is no third category. This is not a menagerie – sheep, goats, cows, chickens. There is one Judge at the end – Jesus. And there are only two kinds of person. All humanity will find itself either as a sheep or a goat. The fates of these two groups are eternal and, on that day, irrevocable.

This is the news Jesus announces and it wakes us up to eternal realities. We spend our time ruminating over other divisions – right-wing or left-wing politics, public or private education, Blackberry or iPhone. But this is the division of eternal significance – sheep or goat. Which are we?

Well let's first notice the asymmetry between the two.

> The sheep *come.* The goats *depart.*
>
> The sheep are blessed *by the Father.* The goats are simply cursed.
>
> The sheep *inherit* the kingdom. The goats just 'go away.'
>
> The kingdom is prepared *for the sheep.* Eternal punishment is prepared for *the devil and his angels.*

From this passage it is clear that heaven is for people, hell is for devils. The only reason people end up in hell is that, insanely, they follow the devil to *his* fate. Hell is not *for* people. It is the greatest tragedy in the world that *people* end up there. But they *do* end up there. And so Christ warns us.

It is important to notice this asymmetrical nature to the blessing and cursing. The Father personally blesses the sheep. The goats simply *are* cursed. And standing in between them is Jesus. He defines the future. Eternity pivots on Christ – it is 'coming to' or 'departing from' Him that carries eternal significance.

Before we examine the characteristics of the sheep and goats, let's note one more fact about them. They are sheep and goats *before* Jesus describes any of their actions. They are on the right and left *before* He points to any of their deeds. Their actions merely demonstrate their nature. There is nothing that the sheep or goats did *in order to become* sheep or goats. Indeed both the sheep and the goats were entirely unaware of what they were doing or failing to do. Neither grouping acted to *become* sheep or goats. They simply couldn't help acting *as* sheep and goats.

So what are these groups like? Jesus says to the sheep:

> "I was an hungred, and ye gave me meat: I was thirsty, and ye gave me drink: I was a stranger, and ye took me in: Naked, and ye clothed me: I was sick, and ye visited me: I was in prison, and ye came unto me." (Matthew 25:35-36)

They are such Christ-like acts. Feeding, sheltering, healing, comforting. These sheep are very like their Shepherd. Yet Jesus does not say they did it "like me" or "for the sake of me." He says they did it "*to* me." How is that possible? That's the question the sheep ask:

> "Then shall the righteous answer him, saying, Lord, when saw we thee an hungred, and fed thee? or thirsty, and gave thee drink? When saw we thee a stranger, and took thee in? or naked, and

> clothed thee? Or when saw we thee sick, or in prison, and came unto thee? And the King shall answer and say unto them, Verily I say unto you, Inasmuch as ye have done it unto one of the least of these my brethren, ye have done it unto me."
> (Matthew 25:37-40)

Christ is hidden in the least of His brethren. Acts of Christ-like mercy directed to the family of Jesus are kindnesses to Christ Himself. Just as He takes the persecution of His people personally (Acts 9:4), so He takes the care of His people personally.

It is a wonderful thought that the smallest acts of mercy – acts that we have long forgotten – are remembered by Jesus the Judge. On the other hand the goats are characterised by their callous indifference to the needs of Christ's people.

Jesus says to them:

> "I was an hungred, and ye gave me no meat: I was thirsty, and ye gave me no drink: I was a stranger, and ye took me not in: naked, and ye clothed me not: sick, and in prison, and ye visited me not. Then shall they also answer him, saying, Lord, when saw we thee an hungred, or athirst, or a stranger, or naked, or sick, or in prison, and did not minister unto thee? Then shall he answer them, saying, Verily I say unto you, Inasmuch as ye did it not to one of the least of these, ye did it not to me."
> (Matthew 25:42-45)

Here is perhaps the most striking difference between the sheep and the goats: the sheep can't remember when they did any good, the goats can't remember when they didn't! The sheep are entirely forgetful of the works they have performed. It is the goats that are mindful of their deeds (and indignant that they should be found wanting). The sheep have *found* righteousness in their Shepherd and unthinkingly express it to His brethren. The goats *assert* their righteousness to the Shepherd yet are unthinking towards His people.

Jesus is not laying out a programme of works for those who would earn heaven. Those who end up in the kingdom seem blissfully unaware of any "merit". And the works that are mentioned have nothing "religious" about them. Those trying to climb the ladder to impress the Judge have forgotten what the Judge has done. He has stooped down to the very depths. He comes to us in grace, transforms us into little christs, then puts Himself into our neighbours and says, "Come away from the ladder, come out into the world, that's where I am. I am always coming down. And my love is for spreading!" His life of self-emptying love is contagious. And wonderfully – according to this parable – it is the life of the *eternal* kingdom.

13 October – John 13:1-38

Foot washing

How are you known by those around you? What would they describe you?

Busy? Easy-going? Nice? Withdrawn? Driven? Glum?

What about your church? How is it known in your area?

The night before Jesus died He spoke of *one* mark by which His followers are to be identified in the world. One word should spring to mind when the world thinks about Christians. Loving.

> "A new commandment I give unto you, That ye love one another; as I have loved you, that ye also love one another. By this shall all men know that ye are my disciples, if ye have love one to another." (John 13:34-35)

The distinguishing mark of the Christian is not a dress code, not an institutional configuration, not even primarily a doctrinal or moral or religious code. The ultimate, distinguishing mark of the Christ-follower is love.

This is not simply Jesus' last request. Jesus calls it a new command. 'New' because it is to be taken up afresh in every generation. But this is not a suggestion from Jesus. It's a command: *As* He has loved us, so we love one another.

This speaks of manner, of order and of movement.

Manner: We are to love in the same manner as Christ has loved us.

Order: We are to love *having been loved* by Christ.

Movement: We are not to "return the favour" to Jesus but to "pass it on."

All of this is taught in the foot washing which provides the backdrop to this teaching.

In John 13 it is the night before Jesus' death. And just when you might expect Jesus to be comforted and supported by His followers, it is Jesus who pours Himself out for them:

> "When Jesus knew that his hour was come that he should depart out of this world unto the Father, having loved his own which were in the world, he loved them unto the end… Jesus knowing that the Father had given all things into his hands, and that he was come from God, and went to God; He riseth from supper, and laid aside his garments; and took a towel, and girded himself. After that he poureth water into a bason, and began to wash the disciples' feet…" (John 13:1,3-5)

Here is Jesus 'loving unto the end.' And the foot washing parallels His own history as Son of God. Just as He left the Father's side to love us in costly, sacrificial service, so He leaves His place at the table, trades His robe for a towel and washes His disciples.

And once He had washed and dried their feet, He took up the robe again and returned to His place. In verse 12 He asks, "Know ye what I have done to you?"

Do they? And do we? This foot washing is a picture of something far deeper. Jesus had come from God, was returning to God, and the route which He trod took Him to the utter depths of the cross. We must never forget that these hands which lovingly washed His friends' feet would, in a matter of hours, be nailed to a Roman cross. We cannot forget this because the washing is meant to picture Christ's love shown at the cross.

And what a picture! The ruler of the universe, stooping and serving His followers.

John writes about it recalling every last detail. Verse 5:

> "After that he poureth water into a bason, and began to wash the disciples' feet, and to wipe them with the towel wherewith he was girded."

As John writes about it, he is carried back to the moment it happened. John was there. He'd had his own feet personally washed and padded dry by the LORD of all creation.

How would you feel as Jesus came around the table to you?

I was once in India, staying with a very respectable family in Indian society. The father was a Nawab – the equivalent of a Maharajah or the British equivalent of a Lord. And while I was there, my hosts were insisting that I had a pedicure. I flatly refused – no way was I going to let someone poke around my carbuncled monstrosities. I didn't want to stand over another human being while they fussed over my dirty feet. No person should have to do that. It is such an awkward thing, to have someone hold your naked feet, to wash water over them and towel them dry while all you can do is sit there and watch. There is something very uncomfortable about allowing someone to serve you to that level.

But I was uncomfortable having one of the household servants do it. It is unthinkable to imagine my host – this Lord – taking off *his* royal robes, wrapping a towel around *his* waist and kneeling at my stinking feet.

That is inconceivable for us. But what about this? In John 13, the Lord of the universe does this very thing.

This is how Jesus has loved His disciples. He loves them in action. He loves in concrete service. He addresses their needs. He loves in humility. He gives up His rights and privileges. He loves in a costly way. He loves even under pressure – the cross was just hours away! He loves unconditionally – these men would, by the end of the night, betray Him, desert Him or deny Him. Yet He lovingly washes *all* their feet, even Judas'. And He loves in self-forgetfulness – He doesn't care that He loses face. He is not concerned for His own self-image.

How do we measure up to Christ's new command?

I can kid myself that I'm loving… until it means inconvenience, or a loss of face, or until my love is not returned in kind. And how often does our love evaporate when we're under pressure from other quarters?

But notice again the order – *as* Christ has loved us, so we love others. There's an order in which we are to obey the new command. First *be* loved. *Then* love. First *receive* Jesus' love. Then pass it on. First know, realise, appreciate – then do. First understand, then act. That's the order.

In fact this order is one that Jesus Himself follows. Did you notice that very strange line in verse 3? In verse 3 we get a rare psychological commentary on the thought-life of Jesus:

> "Jesus knowing that the Father had given all things into his hands, and that he was come from God, and went to God; He riseth from supper…" (John 13:3)

Jesus loved the world out of the security He already had from His Father. He first received love and *then* passed it on. If that's the order for the Son of God, we certainly cannot short-circuit the process.

Peter thinks he can. Peter wants to put his own *doing* ahead of Christ's love. As Jesus comes around with the bowl Peter protests:

> "Thou shalt never wash my feet." (John 13:8)

Later on Peter commits the same error. In verse 37 he boldly proclaims:

> "I will lay down my life for thy sake."

He has things backwards: "Don't wash my feet, I'll wash yours… Don't die for me, I'll die for you."

Jesus has to burst his bubble in v38. Peter has no resources to play the part of Jesus. He will deny Christ before the night is out. That's a shocking turn-around for a man who sounds so spiritual, so committed. But actually Peter's words in the upper room are full of the same independent self-assuredness which lead him to *deny* Jesus.

Peter's mistake in a nut-shell was this: he trusted in his own love for Jesus rather than Jesus' love for him. He reversed the order. He put his own acts of love ahead of Christ's. And when the crunch came, of course his own love failed.

Will we submit to the humbling, sacrificial love of Christ? He stoops not just to our feet but to a cross. But through it, we are cleansed and ready to serve.

14 October – John 14:1-4; 17:20-26

In my Father's house are many mansions

What lies beyond death?

The Hindu might claim reincarnation. The Muslim seeks a paradise, with Allah conspicuous by his absence. The atheist asserts there is nothing. What is the Christian hope?

In words that are read out at funerals the world over, Jesus says this:

> "Let not your heart be troubled: ye believe in God, believe also in me. In my Father's house are many mansions: if it were not so, I would have told you. I go to prepare a place for you. And if I go and prepare a place for you, I will come again, and receive you unto myself; that where I am, there ye may be also."
> (John 14:1-3)

First let's examine two phrases that can send people on wild goose chases of interpretation. The word for "mansions" is difficult to translate. It occurs only one other time in the Bible – in this very chapter: "If a man love me, he will keep my words: and my Father will love him, and we will come unto him, and make our ***abode*** with him." (John 14:23) Perhaps, therefore, it's best to understand verse 2 as something like "In my Father's household, there are many abodes." Jesus' point is not about the architecture of our eternal habitation (extensions necessitated after every conversion!). He is telling us about the roominess of the Father's household. Always space for more!

The other phrase that can give the wrong impression is in verse 3: "I go and prepare a place." This does not refer to some celestial renovations Jesus has to make before our rooms are ready. Our place is not prepared by a team of angelic property developers. No, it *is* the going of Jesus that prepares our place. Jesus is speaking of the cross. His departure is His death on Calvary. That's what secures our place.

So now that we have cleared the ground, what do we positively learn about our eternal hope? Just this: our hope is Christ Himself:

> "I will come again, and receive you unto myself; that where I am, there ye may be also." (John 14:3)

Here is the whole purpose of Christ's coming. He is the One who was "with God in the beginning" (John 1:2). The Greek puts it more literally that Christ was *towards* the Father from eternity. He faces His Father and is ever drawn to Him, seeing His face (John 6:46) and resting in His bosom (John 1:18).

What then is salvation? It is being drawn by the Spirit of God into the Son of God, that He might bring us to where He is. As He prays in John 17:24:

> "Father, I will that they also, whom thou hast given me, be with me where I am; that they may behold my glory, which thou hast given me: for thou lovedst me before the foundation of the world."

Eternal life is something that begins the minute we trust Christ, but it will be consummated in face-to-face fullness when we see Him. This destiny is to be *with Jesus* and therefore to participate in *His* life of loving fellowship with the Father and by the Spirit.

What will that look like? Well John 13 gives us a picture…

It was a good meal, good friends, good wine. People were relaxing around the table. One man seemed even more relaxed than the rest. We are told:

> "Now there was leaning on Jesus' bosom one of his disciples, whom Jesus loved… He then lying on Jesus' breast [asked him a question]" (John 13:23-25)

Here, we assume, is John himself – the author of this Gospel. As he tells the story he remembers leaning back against Jesus. Hearing His heart-beat. Listening to His breathing. John was one of the younger if not the youngest disciple. And he calls himself "the beloved disciple." Clearly he felt completely at ease with Jesus – leaning back on his chest. Jesus had just washed their feet. He was teaching them about His Father and because it was Passover they would have been singing hymns around the dinner table. We can imagine, throughout, Jesus' arm around His young friend as John leant back on Jesus.

John knew he could find rest, peace and welcome in the bosom of Jesus. And Jesus is the One who has eternal rest, peace and welcome in the bosom of the Father. Those few minutes around the dinner table are a picture of our everlasting hope. Those beloved of Jesus are invited into His arms as He rests secure in the Father's.

No other view of the afterlife comes close to the *personal* hope of the Christian. Other religions may go into detail about the pleasures of paradise, but for Christians the focus is different. Christ is our life and He is our hope. Whatever else the future holds, this is the heart of it – warm, personal, feasting joy in the company of Christ, the Heavenly Bridegroom. Therefore, "Let not your heart be troubled".

15 October – John 14:5-31

I am the Way, the Truth and the Life

– "That's the way."

– "Ain't that the truth."

– "This is the life."

How do we tend to speak of the way, the truth and the life?

For us, 'the way' is usually a technique or learned habit. In the 'religious realm' we might think of lengthy pilgrimages and ritualised approaches to God.

For us, 'the truth' is information or compelling logic. In the 'religious realm' we might think of the mysteries of the faith or catechisms which must be taught.

For us, 'the life' is ordering drinks poolside on our summer holiday, or walking through breath-taking scenery. In the 'religious realm' we might think of the life as something far-off – an eternal reward for those who get 'the way' and 'the truth' right.

The trouble with our thinking is that we leave Jesus out of it. And the results are disastrous.

In John 14, Jesus has just redefined the afterlife for His followers. The essence of our future hope is that we will be where Jesus is. The future is not a paradise of pleasures so much as the *presence* of Jesus.

Jesus will similarly *personalise* our concepts of way and truth and life as He continues…

> "And whither I go ye know, and the way ye know. Thomas saith unto him, Lord, we know not whither thou goest; and how can we know the way? Jesus saith unto him, **I am the way, the truth, and the life**: no man cometh unto the Father, but by me. If ye had known me, ye should have known my Father also: and from henceforth ye know him, and have seen him. Philip saith unto him, Lord, show us the Father, and it sufficeth us. Jesus saith unto him, Have I been so long time with you, and yet hast thou not known me, Philip? He that hath seen me hath seen the Father; and how sayest thou then, Show us the Father? Believest thou not that I am in the Father, and the Father in me?"
> (John 14:4-10)

What is the way to God?

It is not a long ascent to heaven through deeds and rituals. The way is Jesus. And therefore it is a way that has come down to us! The way is not *our* approach to God. The way is Christ's approach to God and He is given freely to us.

This means if we ask ourselves "Am I on the way to God?" we are really asking the question "Am I in Jesus?" And if we are in Jesus, we are not just on the way – we have arrived! Jesus does not show us the way and leave us to get on with it. Jesus blazes the trail and invites us directly to the destination.

What is the truth of God?

It is not an impersonal logic that we have to piece together through information gathered 'on the ground.' The truth is Jesus. Therefore, again, the truth has come down to us and told us what we didn't already know.

This means if we ask ourselves "Do I *know* God?" we are really asking the question "Do I see Jesus for who He is?" This is how He speaks to Philip. When Philip wants to see God, Jesus insists "Look at me!" Jesus does not show us truths about God, He puts Himself in our eye-line and says "Keep looking." Truth does not assess the claims of Jesus. Jesus is the Truth who assesses everything else!

What is the life of God?

It is not an abstract ethical programme or spiritual state or future bliss. The life of God *is* Jesus. The Son constitutes (in fact eternally constitutes) the Father as Father. And life is to be drawn into Christ, to share in *His* life with God. As Jesus prays in John 17:3:

> "This is life eternal, that they might know thee the only true God, and Jesus Christ, whom thou hast sent."

Jesus does not simply get us to God or get us to truth or get us to eternal life. He *is* those things. Those things – even the Father and the Spirit! – are *in* Jesus. He contains, within Himself, God on the one hand and all creation on the other.

How do you think of Jesus?

You cannot think too highly of Him. He is incomparable and all-encompassing.

How do you think of God and the world?

You cannot think of them Christ-lessly. He's got the whole world in His hands!

16 October – John 15:1-12

I am the Vine, ye are the branches

Last time we saw the incomparable enormity of Jesus. He is the Way, the Truth and the Life. If we want to see God we must look no further but only *at* Jesus. For, as He says, "The Father is in me and I am in the Father." (John 14:10)

While we are still reeling from this truth, Jesus hits us with another. And this time it's personal.

In John 15 verse 9 Jesus makes the most astonishing claim:

> "As the Father hath loved me, so have I loved you."

Ask yourself – how has the Father loved the Son?

He has loved Him perfectly, unbreakably, begininglessly and endlessly. Remember from John 14 that Jesus is so much one with the Father that they are *in* each other. As we have seen, Jesus is "in the bosom of the Father" (John 1:18). Their love is the original love that both predated and produced the universe. And now Jesus says that this love overflows to *me*. How is that possible?

It's possible only because of "union with Christ." We share in the eternal love of God because we share in Christ Himself. The believer is one with Jesus, even as Jesus is one with the Father. And perhaps the most evocative description of this one-ness is in John 15:1-8. Here Jesus says:

> "**I am the vine, ye are the branches**" (John 15:5)

Throughout the Old Testament Israel is pictured as a vine. But for the most part it is a fruitless vine. Now it's true that some trees have a use apart from their fruitfulness – perhaps they are good for furniture or timber. But not vines. If a vine is fruitless, it is useful only as firewood. This is our natural state, cut off from the life of God, fruitless before him and good for nothing.

But step forward Jesus. He is the true Vine. He is the true people of God, the true humanity. Unlike natural man, Jesus has a connection to the ultimate Life-source and brings forth much fruit. And the good news is this: we are grafted in to the fruitful Vine and we have life in Him. Now that we are *in* Jesus we are *in* on the beloved Son as He stands in the Niagara of the Father's love.

Just think of how close the believer is to Jesus. He doesn't simply say "I am the root structure, you are the vine." Or "I am the trunk, you are the branches." Jesus is the whole vine and we are branches within that vine. Jesus comprehends His people in a remarkable way. He incorporates us into Himself such that we are a part of Him.

We are one with Jesus like a bride with her groom, like a body with its head, like a branch with its vine. We do not have a separate existence from Jesus. We cannot pursue our life, our identity, our flourishing apart from Jesus. And for His part, Jesus cannot reject us, abandon us or deny us any more than He can reject, abandon or deny Himself.

Who He is, we become. Where He is, we dwell. What He has, we inherit. What He's done, we possess. We are one with Jesus and He is one with the Father. Therefore it really is true what He says: "As the Father hath loved me, so have I loved you."

Is this the reality you dwell upon day to day? Jesus tells us, 10 times in 7 verses to "abide" in Him. We are to make our home in Jesus. To remain in this love, this truth, this Vine, this Jesus. A thousand things will distract us in our day. A thousand competing abodes will offer a sense of security and identity. But none of them compare to Christ.

> "Abide in me, and I in you. As the branch cannot bear fruit of itself, except it abide in the vine; no more can ye, except ye abide in me. **I am the vine, ye are the branches**: He that abideth in

me, and I in him, the same bringeth forth much fruit."
(John 15:4-5)

17 October – John 15:13-27

Greater love hath no man than this …

War memorials the world over record these words from Jesus:

> "**Greater love hath no man than this, that a man lay down his life for his friends.**" (John 15:13)

In the context of a war memorial we might picture a brave soldier taking a bullet for another. Or perhaps throwing himself on a grenade, or stretchering out an injured comrade under heavy fire. If we were the one saved, we would be eternally grateful.

But when Jesus originally spoke these words, He was telling us that we *are* the saved ones. Therefore *we* are His friends. And He is the one who takes the bullet. Out of immense love, Jesus comes to the fight, joins us in our predicament and lays down His life for us.

Over the past few days we have been speaking of the eternal love of God. But in John 15 we see this love earthed into the blood, sweat and tears of our own fallen state.

And that is absolutely essential. Because someone reading the last few posts might well object to this lofty talk about God's love. It's all very well, they may protest, to speak of the life of the Trinity before the world began. It's all very well to speak of our mystical union with Christ. It's all very well to speak of our participation, through Christ, in the eternal love of God. But how on earth does that love meet with me in my sin and suffering, my curse and condemnation? The answer that Jesus gives is that it meets us at the cross.

This great love, about which Christ has been speaking for the last three chapters, does not and cannot remain a heavenly love. It must descend to our situation. Which means it enters into even our hellish cut-off-ness from the life of God. Jesus comes into the trenches, takes up our cause and faces the fire.

Having taken us into Himself, the True Vine is consumed on the cross (Psalm 80:14-19), taking the judgement that belongs to us. This is how He loves His friends.

To believe in an abstract love from heaven is not enough for us. When we know the depths of our own depravity, our consciences are not placated by imagining some benign smile from above. We need to know that God's love is a *knowing* love, a divine "nevertheless". Before He declares His oaths, we need to know that He sees us to the bottom – that His love does not skim over but actually plumbs the depths of our sin. But this is precisely what the cross tells us.

There can be no greater love than this. Our Heavenly Friend does not forget about our unloveliness – He enters into it, He endures it and its consequences, and He rises again to say "Even so, I have loved you with eyes wide open, I have loved you at your very worst, and I have loved you more than my own life. Nothing can separate you from my love."

> "But God commendeth his love toward us, in that, while we were yet sinners, Christ died for us. Much more then, being now justified by his blood, we shall be saved from wrath through him. For if, when we were enemies, we were reconciled to God by the death of his Son, much more, being reconciled, we shall be saved by his life." (Romans 5:8-10)

18 October – Matthew 26:17-30

Jesus took bread, and blessed it, and brake it …

Every Sunday for 2000 years ministers of the gospel have been repeating this phrase.

All over the world, Christ's people gather to eat the bread and drink the wine and they hear these words:

> "And as they were eating, Jesus took bread, and blessed it, and brake it, and gave it to the disciples, and said, Take, eat…" (Matthew 26:26)

Let's consider each phrase…

As they were eating…

The Lord's Supper is a *supper*. It is a meal. And this is how salvation is portrayed throughout the Bible. God's people are not promised a heavenly buffet – finger food that we can take poolside while we top up our tan. We are called to a feast – a wedding feast with Christ as host. We are brought into the heart of the Family, to sit at table and dine with our Lord. There could be no greater sign of our fellowship with God than that we are invited to eat with Him.

… Jesus took bread…

As we will see, Jesus says of this bread: "This is my body." Here is how the feast comes about. Before Jesus is the Host, He becomes the main course. In history, the Son of God did indeed take a body. He took our flesh, entering our humanity and making it His own.

… and blessed it…

Jesus lived perfectly before the Father. And the law set out many blessings for full obedience (Deuteronomy 28:1-14). Therefore Jesus comes into our situation and lives the blessed life in our place. Yet now, at the end of His life, something else happens…

… and brake it…

The violence of the act is shocking. This bread is torn apart in front of the disciples. Here we see the cross dramatised. Now, instead of the blessings of Christ's obedient life, we remember the curses Jesus takes for *our* disobedience to the law (Galatians 3:13; Deuteronomy 28:15-29:29). The blessed One is broken. But He is broken for us…

… and gave it to the disciples.

What is the whole purpose of Christ's taking flesh, of living the blessed life and dying the cursed death? That we might take and eat. Jesus wants to feed us with His very Self. Here is the self-giving love of Christ – to be torn apart to bring life to the world.

So then, as it says in the Book of Common Prayer: "Take and eat this in remembrance that Christ died for thee, and feed on him in thy heart by faith with thanksgiving."

19 October – Matthew 26:26-29; 1 Corinthians 10:14-17

This is my body

The mission of Christ's life was His death. It was His 'glory', or His 'hour' as He kept calling it. And on the night before He died He instituted a meal to commemorate this central act of His coming.

Incredibly, Jesus did not mainly set Himself forth as the *Host* of this meal (although He is – it's the *Lord's* supper after all). But more fundamentally, Jesus offers Himself as the main course.

He takes bread, gives thanks, breaks it and gives it to His disciples saying "**This is my body**." (Matthew 26:26).

The meaning of His death is contained in this little phrase. Jesus, torn apart like bread, is given that we might live. He is devoured, that we might be fed. He is broken that we might be nourished.

To be eaten up is a common way of speaking about death. For instance, the Psalmist speaks of his deadly foes like this:

> "When the wicked, even mine enemies and my foes, came upon me to eat up my flesh, they stumbled and fell." (Psalm 27:2)

When a person eats the flesh of another they take advantage of their death. And so Jesus wants us to do with *His* death. He wants us to take advantage of His sacrifice. In fact the Old Testament sacrifices *were* eaten after they were killed. *First* they turned away wrath, then they nourished and provided an occasion for fellowship. The Passover Lamb was the same – first its blood shielded from judgement, then it sustained the people for their journey out of Egypt.

And so it is with Jesus. He is our propitiation *and* our fellowship meal. He's given *for us* as our atoning sacrifice and given *to us* as our ongoing sustenance. Jesus really is the Bread of life. And it's His death that brings us life.

Think of a loaf torn apart and handed to you. Freely offered. Life-giving. Hunger-satisfying. Fellowship-creating. Generous. Nourishing. Available. That is Jesus for you. Because of His once-for-all death on that Friday, He says to us today:

> "This is my body which is given for you." (Luke 22:19)

20 October – Matthew 26:26-29; 1 Corinthians 11:17-33

This is my blood

In 2 Thessalonians 2, the Apostle Paul speaks of "the lie." It's a deception which the human race falls for every time. Essentially the lie is this: We believe that the Lord is grudging. We imagine that, if He's gracious at all, He doles out blessings with a teaspoon.

Ever since Satan first spoke to Eve he has been peddling this same deception: "You mean to tell me God's withholding all this fruit from you? What a miser!" Eve fell for it. Adam fell for it. The world falls for it. Every day. And so do I.

The greatest battle in my Christian life is to fight "the lie." Every day I am tempted to view God as a distant, tight-fisted, kill-joy. It makes me mistrust Him, shut down and close off from Him. Then I try to manage life out of my own resources. This lie will kill my spiritual life.

So how should I fight the lie? With the blood of Christ.

After handing out bread at the last supper…

> "Jesus took the cup, and gave thanks, and gave it to them, saying, Drink ye all of it; For this is my blood of the new testament, which is shed for many for the remission of sins." (Matthew 26: 27-28)

It's a shocking dramatisation of the cross. Bread torn apart – *this is my body.* Red wine poured out – *this is my blood.* Jesus would be utterly consumed and exhausted on the cross. Broken and expended… *for us.* That's the whole point – it's for *us.* Jesus takes death, we get the feast. He gives His blood, we get the banquet.

And just think of what blood means in the Bible. In Leviticus 17 the LORD speaks of the blood of the sacrifices:

> "The life of the flesh is in the blood: and I have given it to you upon the altar to make an atonement for your souls: for it is the blood that maketh an atonement for the soul." (Leviticus 17:11)

To pour out blood is to pour out life. And this is what Jesus does for us. He gives His infinitely precious blood – the blood of God (Acts 20:28) – in atonement for *our* souls.

Who can look to the cross and doubt the generosity of our Lord? Here is no grudging miser. Here is Life expended to the very last drop. Here is a gushing forth of self that we might live.

This God does not dispense blessings with a teaspoon. He pours Him*self* out – for us and to us. At the cross, 'the lie' is unmasked. Satan is the miser. We are the selfish ones. God is Giver – though it cost Him everything. And He doesn't merely give us *things,* He pours out His own blood. He expends Himself in complete self-offering. And all we can do is gratefully receive.

21 October – Mark 14:32-42

Abba, Father

It's one of the first sounds a baby will make. 'Ma ma ma ma'. Or 'Ba ba ba ba'. Which is why, in so many languages, the proud parents take their babbling children to be speaking their names. 'Mama' or 'Amma' is a very common word for 'mother'. And 'Papa' or 'Baba' is similarly common as a word for father. In Aramaic it's "Abba" which a child will call their father from the very earliest age.

Yet the name is not only reserved for childhood (as "Daddy" might be in English). The toddler who cries "Abba", will continue to call their father "Abba" long into adulthood. It is not only an intimate term, but one of respect.

But here's the question: Who gets to call God Most High "Abba"?

If I called the Queen "Liz" that would be a gross dishonour, but at least such familiarity makes no *claim* on the Queen. I have no *right* to call her "Liz" but in doing so I haven't established any claim to her throne or right to protection or provision. "Liz" is intimate but it doesn't set me in a particular relationship to her. But if I claim to be family, that's something else entirely. If the Queen were not only Ma'am but also Mum, that would put me in a very privileged position. As *family* I am in on what she is in on. As family I can inherit.

So let's return to our question: Who gets to call God Most High "Abba"? Answer: the Son of God. And, really, *only* Him. Only Jesus can articulate that degree of intimacy. Only Jesus can make that kind of claim on the God of Heaven.

In the New Testament we read three "Abba, Father"s. The first is in the garden of Gethsemane (of which, more tomorrow). There Jesus prays in blood earnestness to His Father as He contemplates the cross. The obedient Son call out to the Father with a title that *only* the obedient Son can.

And yet, the phrase is used twice more by the Apostle Paul.

In Galatians 4:6 he writes:

> "God hath sent forth the Spirit of his Son into your hearts, crying, Abba, Father." (Galatians 4:6)

Here we see the Spirit sweeping up the believer into the perfect prayer-life of the Son. The Spirit of Christ prays Christ's prayer in us and through us. We are drawn by the Spirit *into* the union and communion which the obedient Son enjoys with His Abba, Father. The believer's new heart-beat is "Abba, Father, Abba, Father, Abba, Father" because the Spirit is making that cry from deep within us.

But not only this, Romans 8:15 says:

> "ye have received the Spirit of adoption, whereby *we* cry, Abba, Father."

"Abba, Father" is no longer just what the Son prays. And it's not just what the Spirit of the Son prays *in* us. The Spirit now teaches us to pray "Abba, Father" for ourselves.

What right do we have to call the King of Kings "Daddy"? None. Not in ourselves. But Christ has that right. And by His Spirit, He shares that right with us.

As Mike Reeves has said: "To be the son of a millionaire would be nice. To be the firstborn of some wealthy king would be wonderful enough. But we are the beloved children of the Emperor of the Universe." And we can call Him "Abba, Father."

> "Behold, what manner of love the Father hath bestowed upon us, that we should be called the sons of God." (1 John 3:1)

22 October – Matthew 26:36-46

Let this cup pass from me

It was the original poisoned chalice. Just minutes after pouring wine into a cup of blessing, Jesus prays to His Abba, Father regarding a very different cup:

> Jesus kneeled down, and prayed, Saying, Father, if thou be willing, remove this cup from me: nevertheless not my will, but thine, be done. And there appeared an angel unto him from heaven, strengthening him. And being in an agony he prayed more earnestly: and his sweat was as it were great drops of blood falling down to the ground. (Luke 22:41-44)

In Matthew 26:39 we read the more familiar version of His prayer: "**let this cup pass from me**." He took the cup of the upper room gladly, He fervently wishes away *this* cup.

Between these two cups we learn something of the "wonderful exchange" which takes place between Christ and the believer.

One cup was offered in the upper room. One cup was offered in the Garden of Gethsemane.

One cup is given to us. One cup Jesus drinks for Himself.

One cup is for the forgiveness of sins. One cup is full of wrath and judgement.

One cup brings life. One cup brings death.

One cup is described as a cup of blessing. The other cup is a cup of curse.

Yet Jesus takes the curses that we might have the blessings. He drinks what we deserve so that we receive what only He deserves.

And though this exchange is offered for free. It is unfathomably costly for Christ.

Consider how the bible speaks of this cup of judgement:

> "In the hand of the LORD there is a cup, and the wine is red; it is full of mixture; and he poureth out of the same: but the dregs thereof, all the wicked of the earth shall wring them out, and drink them." (Psalm 75:8)

> "Thus saith the LORD God of Israel unto me; Take the wine cup of this fury at my hand, and cause all the nations, to whom I send thee, to drink it. And they shall drink, and be moved, and be mad, because of the sword that I will send among them. Then took I the cup at the LORD's hand, and made all the nations to drink, unto whom the LORD had sent me… Therefore thou shalt say unto them, Thus saith the LORD of hosts, the God of Israel; Drink ye, and be drunken, and spue, and fall, and rise no more, because of the sword which I will send among you. And it shall be, if they refuse to take the cup at thine hand to drink, then shalt thou say unto them, Thus saith the LORD of hosts; Ye shall certainly drink. For, lo, I begin to bring evil on the city which is called by my name, and should ye be utterly unpunished? Ye shall not be unpunished: for I will call for a sword upon all the inhabitants of the earth, saith the LORD of hosts."
> (Jeremiah 25:15-29)

> "If any man worship the beast and his image, and receive his mark in his forehead, or in his hand, The same shall drink of the wine of the wrath of God, which is poured out without mixture into the cup of his indignation; and he shall be tormented with fire and brimstone in the presence of the holy angels, and in the presence of the Lamb." (Revelation 14:9-10)

This is why Jesus was "exceeding sorrowful, even unto death." This is why He asks for the cup to pass from Him. This is why Luke's gospel records that "his sweat was as it were great drops of blood falling down to the ground." (Luke 22:44). Blood vessels are bursting all over His body as He contemplates drinking this cup. It is full of the furious wrath of God.

The cross is not a three-hour inconvenience for the Son of God. It means entering into the infinite abyss of sin and curse. The hell of the cross was not easier for Christ than the hell of the damned. The hell of the cross was worse. All hell was distilled in that cup. All hell converged on that cross. And for the holy Son of God it was not *more* bearable but infinitely worse. Therefore He *wanted* another way. Of *course* He prays that the cup might pass.

And yet, how strange that He should pray it. Here is the Lamb slain from the foundation of the world (Revelation 13:8). But as that dreaded hour draws near, He seeks earnestly for another path. How terrible is the godforsakenness of the cross! And yet how necessary.

Often people question the necessity of the cross. *Why should Christ have to die? Why doesn't God simply forgive? Why this business with blood sacrifice? Surely there's another way!?*

These are all questions which, in principle, Christ Himself asks here in the garden. This is the very essence of His hour-long wrestling. And yet His Abba, Father provides no other way. There is no cup of blessing for us unless Christ takes the cup of curse. We cannot escape from the furnace of judgement unless Christ goes for us. The cup of wrath cannot pass from us unless it passes to Christ.

And here in the garden, Man steps in for man. Where Adam had failed in that first garden, Christ triumphs. He rises from prayer resolved "Thy will be done!" (v39). He has faced the prospect in all its horror – either He goes to hell or we do. And He comes to His decision: "Father, let it be me!"

> *Amazing love, how can it be?*
> *That Thou my God shouldst die for me!*

23 October – Matthew 26:36-46

The Spirit is willing, the flesh is weak

My teenage years were haunted by Gethsemane. For a serious-minded 14 year old, this was the ultimate display of godly devotion. Here was Christ leading the way in the school of prayer – showing us how to "give it all up for God." In desperation He prostrates Himself before the Father, He pours out His soul, He offers *everything* to God no matter the cost and declares "thy will be done!"

Well then, what's a good Christian boy to do but follow in His footsteps? So that's what I tried. Night after night, year after year I prayed what I considered to be "Gethsemane prayers." "God take me, use me, come into my life, have it all, **your will be done!**"

I expected heaven to open, or perhaps angels to attend me. At least a funny feeling in my stomach, some sign that I'd been heard. But I got nothing. So I prayed again. This time more fervently. Still nothing. So I decided to pull out all the stops. I went outside at dead of night, the way Jesus did. I would find the scariest clearing in a forest and fall prostrate before God: "Take me, use me, your will be done!" And the response from heaven? Nothing.

After a thousand of such prayers I came to the conclusion that God didn't want me. So I didn't want Him. I left home to have as good a time as possible without Him.

Yet a few years later the Lord brought me back through this same passage. Our Bible study came to Luke 22 and I said how daunted I was by Gethsemane.

> "Daunted? Why?" asked the leader.
>
> "Well," I replied, "I just don't think I can pray Gethsemane prayers the way Jesus did. I don't have that level of commitment."
>
> "The way Jesus did? Glen, who do you think you are in this story?"

I didn't like to say but, well, surely I'm Jesus in the story. Or I'm meant to be anyway.

The leader corrected me. "Do you know who you are? You're Peter."

And the penny dropped. I'm not Jesus! I'm Peter. I'm weak, useless, faithless Peter. I ought to pray with Jesus, but I don't. I fail. And as I fail, Jesus prays for me.

By the Spirit, I belong to Jesus. By the Spirit I *want* to follow Christ. But my flesh is from Adam. My flesh is weak. And I'm constantly falling asleep on the watch.

But Jesus prays for me.

That's the meaning of this story. It's the meaning of the Scriptures. I am not the centre, Christ is. I am not the Faithful, Obedient One, Christ is. My hope is not my self-offering to God. My hope is *Christ's* self-offering to God. And while I sleep and fail and flee and even deny Him – Christ is praying for me.

Christopher Idle put it perfectly:

> When you prayed beneath the trees, it was for me, O Lord;
> When you cried upon your knees, how could it be, O Lord?
> When in blood and sweat and tears, you dismissed your final fears
> When you faced the soldier's spears, you stood for me, O Lord.
>
> When their triumph looked complete, it was for me, O Lord,
> When it seemed like your defeat, they could not see, O Lord!
> When you faced the mob alone, you were silent as a stone,
> And a tree became your throne; you came for me, O Lord.
>
> When you stumbled up the road, you walked for me, O Lord,
> When you took your deadly load, that heavy tree, O Lord;
> When they lifted you on high, and they nailed you up to die,
> And when darkness filled the sky, it was for me, O Lord.
>
> When you spoke with kingly power, it was for me, O Lord;
> In that dread and destined hour you made me free, O Lord.
> Earth and heaven heard you shout, death & hell were put to rout,
> For the grave could not hold out; you are for me, O Lord.

24 October – Luke 22:47-53

Betrayed with a kiss

If ever there was a man who could call himself the elect of the elect, it was Judas.

He was not only Jewish, he was, in all probability, from the tribe of Judah. Certainly his name *means* "Judah" – which refers not simply to the southern kingdom of Israel but also to the royal tribe from which Christ Himself was descended. Here was Jesus' own kith and kin. This alone would make him the elect of the elect.

Yet Judas's privileges go even deeper. The Scriptures constantly present him as a close friend of Christ's (Psalm 41:9; 55:12-13; John 13:18-30). He had not only seen the mighty works of Christ, he had *performed* them too, in Jesus' name (Luke 9:1ff). And, of course, he was one of the twelve. Even more, he was chosen as treasurer of the group (John 12:6). In that sense he was the elect of the elect of the elect of the elect.

And yet here is what *this* chosen one does to the Eternally Chosen One:

> "While Jesus yet spake, behold a multitude, and he that was called Judas, one of the twelve, went before them, and drew near unto

> Jesus to kiss him. But Jesus said unto him, Judas, betrayest thou the Son of man with a kiss?" (Luke 22:47-48)

Just hours earlier Jesus had bent down and washed his feet, then fed him, sacramentally, with His own body and blood. Jesus had only ever done Judas good. Yet now He is betrayed. And betrayed with a kiss.

Biblically speaking, a kiss is not only a sign of intimacy and friendship, it's also an act of worship. One of the key biblical words for worship (*proskuneo*) literally means to "kiss towards." Therefore think of Psalm 2 where the kings of the earth are commanded to "worship the LORD" and, in the same breath, to "Kiss the Son" (Psalm 2:10-12). So here is a literal kissing of the Son by a royal Judah-ite. This should be the essence of worship, in fact it's the height of treason.

And this is the Bible's picture of humanity. It was Judas, the elect of the elect, who betrays Jesus. And betrays Him to the best of the best – the Jewish establishment. And they, with the help of the mightiest of the mighty (the Romans) crucify the Lord of Glory.

Humanity does not stand *with* Jesus in His work. No-one gives Jesus a helping hand when He saves the world. Simon "the rock" fails, deserts and denies Him. Judah *himself* betrays Him. And the children of Abraham sentence Him to death. The best that humanity has to offer is not an aid to Jesus – we only cause His death. And the more we lay claim to strength, wisdom and righteousness, the more complicit we seem to be in His murder. It wasn't the worst of humanity that slew the Son of God – it was the best.

This scene shows the truth so starkly: From the outside we see a respectable man of good breeding worshipping the LORD. In fact it's the very betrayal of God. When it comes to salvation, humanity *only* stands in the way of the LORD. And the very best of humanity, appearing with the *best* of intentions, proves utterly traitorous.

25 October – Matthew 26:14-16, 47-56

Thirty pieces of silver

What would motivate Judas to betray the Son of God? Theories abound. Many reconstruct a supposed political radicalism. Perhaps he was disenchanted by Christ's non-violence. Judas, we imagine, had been hoping for an uprising and was so disappointed by Christ's way of peace that he sold Him out.

That's a fascinating supposition. But it's both groundless and redundant. The Bible tells us exactly why Judas betrayed Jesus:

> "Then one of the twelve, called Judas Iscariot, went unto the chief priests, And said unto them, What will ye give me, and I will deliver him unto you? And they covenanted with him for **thirty pieces of silver**. And from that time he sought opportunity to betray him." (Matthew 26:14-16)

Judas loved money. John 12:6 puts it starkly, "he was a thief".

If that doesn't sound sensational enough as a motive, perhaps we have misunderstood Christ's teaching on money:

According to Jesus, we either serve God or money, (i.e. mammon). We either look to the living God or we seek the resources of this world. Of course, with judgement coming we would be a fool to pursue an abundance of possessions. But such fools we are by nature. And our foolish hearts are revealed by our foolish investments in earthly treasure. ("Where your treasure is, there your heart will be also"). Therefore, as mad as it is to value the Son of God at 30 pieces of silver, this is precisely the motive we should expect from Judas.

But what is the meaning of this price?

Centuries earlier, the prophet Zechariah was given thirty pieces of silver – this was the price he was "prised at". (Zechariah 11:13). Though he calls it a "goodly price" he is perhaps being ironic. All he does with this valuation is to throw the money into the house of the LORD where "the potter" would receive it. His feelings are understandable when we remember the legal significance of "thirty pieces of silver".

In Exodus 21 there are rules concerning the keeping of dangerous animals. If you have been negligent and let out an ox who kills a servant then your own life is forfeit. You ought to die but you can ransom yourself from death by paying thirty pieces of silver. In so doing, you, the guilty one, are redeemed and the servant is valued.

Therefore 30 pieces of silver is the value placed on a servant's life, it's an offensively meagre price for a prophet and it provides redemption for the sinner. In all this we see how fitting it is that *this* was the amount of blood money paid to Judas. Jesus is *the* Servant of the LORD, slain at the hands of the beast. He is *the* Prophet, misunderstood and undervalued by His people, but prized by the Potter. And He is the ransom price offered for we the guilty. A ransom, infinitely more precious than silver or gold:

> "Ye know that ye were not redeemed with corruptible things, as silver and gold, from your vain conversation… But with the

precious blood of Christ, as of a lamb without blemish and without spot." (1 Peter 1:18-19)

My kingdom is not of this world

The myth of violence powerfully shapes our view of the world. We imagine that force must be met with greater force if anything is to be achieved. And of course we tell ourselves that the greater force is justified if it's done in the name of some greater good. Most Hollywood blockbusters follow this storyline.

Take, for instance, the highest grossing film of all time. *Avatar* tells the story of a culture clash between greedy imperialists and a nature-loving indigenous people. Yet however different the natives might be portrayed, how do they overcome the nasty invaders? Through a loud and lengthy slug-fest. In a spectacular special-effects battle, the biggest hitters win. And so a wonderfully imaginative beginning concludes with a predictably bloody finale. And on the deepest level it's neither the imperialists nor the natives who win. In the end, violence wins.

The trial of Jesus might look like one more clash between powers. Facing off are two contenders for the title: King of the Jews. But this encounter will subvert everything we know about power struggles.

Pilate claims to rule the Jews as the vice-regent of Rome. Christ claims to rule the Jews as the Vice-Regent of God! But this is not simply a clash of kings, it's a clash of the *kind* of power by which they rule:

> "Then Pilate entered into the judgment hall again, and called Jesus, and said unto him, Art thou the King of the Jews? Jesus answered him, Sayest thou this thing of thyself, or did others tell it thee of me? Pilate answered, Am I a Jew? Thine own nation and the chief priests have delivered thee unto me: what hast thou done? Jesus answered, **My kingdom is not of this world**: if my kingdom were of this world, then would my servants fight, that I should not be delivered to the Jews: but now is my kingdom not from hence." (John 18:33-36)

Pilate rules the way every human rules – with the sword. *His* servants do indeed fight for him. Pilate has the monopoly of violence in his province. He decides who can wield physical force and who cannot. If you cross him, he'll cross you – literally. He'll line the streets with crosses if needs be. And if anyone were to usurp his rule it would be by bringing *more* earthly power. Force would unseat force. And yet even if that occurred, there's one thing that would remain on the throne – force!

But Jesus hasn't come by force to effect a slightly more benevolent reign of violence. Jesus has come to unseat violence itself. His kingdom is not of this world. The kings of this world ask their servants to fight for them. Jesus subverts this kind of kingdom in two ways. First *He* fights for them. Second, the *way* He fights is by losing. He ends the cycle of violence by *taking* the blows and not retaliating.

Here is the cruciform revolution that Jesus brings to the world. The Apostle Paul, reflecting on the meaning of the cross, said this:

> "The foolishness of God is wiser than men; and the weakness of God is stronger than men. For ye see your calling, brethren, how that not many wise men after the flesh, not many mighty, not many noble, are called: But God hath chosen the foolish things of the world to confound the wise; and God hath chosen the weak things of the world to confound the things which are mighty; And base things of the world, and things which are despised, hath God chosen, yea, and things which are not, to bring to nought things that are:" (1 Corinthians 1:25-28)

How does God overcome strength? With weakness! It's absolutely counter-intuitive but two minute's thought reveals its wisdom. Power-plays are not overcome by a show of force! They can only be unseated by the cross. The Lord of Glory undermines all earthly glory by descending beneath it. And through the cross, Christ establishes a kingdom of servants *not* fighters. Won by His cross, we are called not to kill but to be killed, not to over-power with force, but to over-whelm with love. The spreading of Christ's reign ought to look completely different to the spread of any earthly kingdom. It should look like a base and despised people pointing to a weak and foolish Victim. But this is how we confound the mighty. It is the triumph of grace.

27 October – Luke 23:1-25

Crucify him, crucify him

In 1963, Stanley Milgram's experiment asked anonymous participants to deliver increasingly severe electric shocks to subjects in the next room. Unbeknownst to the participants, the shocks were not real. But had they been, they may have been fatal. The great majority of participants delivered the shocks, even though there were screams of great pain from the next room.

In 1971, Philip Zimbardo ran the Stanford Prison Experiment in which participants were divided into guards and prisoners. The guards were given uniforms and had authority over the 'prisoners'. The two week experiment had to be abandoned after 6 days because of rampant abuse of power on the part of the guards. Zimbardo's book on the subject was called "The Lucifer Effect."

Something happens when people lose their individual identities in the crowd, when there seem to be no consequences, when they act *en masse* , when there is a diffusion of responsibility such that there's always *someone else* to carry the can.

There was a very definite "Lucifer effect" when Pilate addressed the people during the trial of Jesus. There was a custom of releasing a prisoner at the feast of Passover. Pilate suggests that it's Jesus who is released. The crowd seem to prefer having a murderer roam free among them…

> "And they cried out all at once, saying, Away with this man [Jesus], and release unto us Barabbas: (Who for a certain sedition made in the city, and for murder, was cast into prison.) Pilate therefore, willing to release Jesus, spake again to them. But they cried, saying, **Crucify him, crucify him**. And he said unto them the third time, Why, what evil hath he done? I have found no cause of death in him: I will therefore chastise him, and let him go. And they were instant with loud voices, requiring that he might be crucified. And the voices of them and of the chief priests prevailed. And Pilate gave sentence that it should be as they required. And he released unto them him that for sedition and murder was cast into prison, whom they had desired; but he delivered Jesus to their will." (Luke 23:18-25)

This was a Passover crowd – drawn from the four corners of Israel. It's highly likely that many in the crowd had been personally healed by Jesus in the last three years. Certainly a good number would have heard His teaching, seen His miracles and known people whose lives had been transformed by Jesus. And yet, you can feel the electricity crackling among the people, "Crucify him! Crucify him!"

On Palm Sunday many churches have a tradition of dramatising the passion narrative, with the congregation taking on the role of "the crowd." The readings always made a huge impact on me as a child. But this line more than any other shook me. It was always the loudest part of an otherwise sombre service. And there we were, *church people*, and we were baying for the blood of Jesus. Imagine actually being in this crowd. They *are* the people of God and the Messiah's fate lies in their hands. They bay for His blood, even though they don't really know *why*. Pilate asks them, but they have no answer. They just seem driven along this mad path to Deicide.

There are no *reasons* for putting the Son of God to death. There is only this primeval urge in the crowd – He must be done away with. This is our sinful condition expressed in its clearest terms. We would rather have a murderer released among us than the Lord of life!

But even in the midst of our terrible sin, a wonderful gospel presentation is seen. Barabbas is a name that means "Son of his father". He is a counterpart to Jesus. A son of a different father whose unrighteousness reveals a different origin. Here is Adam's son – one very much under Lucifer's effect – he who had been a murderer from the beginning. But on this day, in a very real and literal way, Jesus died for him. Jesus, the Innocent, died in the place of Barabbas, the guilty.

And if Barabbas had dared to walk up to Golgotha on that Friday he could have pointed to the middle cross and said "That should have been me. But Jesus died in my place."

Here is the hope for all the sons and daughters of Adam. Here is the hope for all of us who fall under Lucifer's effect. Christ's death was not merely the will of the people (v25). It was His own will. The cross is not simply the proof of our sinfulness, but the offer of His salvation. His incredible love means that He *wants* to die for devils like Barabbas, and devils like you and me. Therefore we too can point to the cross – the cross that we have bayed for! – and declare with wonder:

> "The Son of God loved me and gave Himself for me."
> (Galatians 2:20)

28 October – Matthew 27:11-26

Pilate washed his hands

The trial of Jesus has everything backwards. The Judge of the world is in the dock. The Truth is cross-examined. The Righteous One is pronounced guilty.

As we saw last time, the people act as judge and jury, while at times Pilate seems more like a public defender. Now in this verse, the Governor seeks to abdicate all governance.

> "When Pilate saw that he could prevail nothing, but that rather a tumult was made, he took water, and washed his hands before the multitude, saying, I am innocent of the blood of this just person: see ye to it." (Matthew 27:24)

During the Nuremberg trials, many Nazis sought to blame those higher up in the chain of command for their crimes. Pilate does the reverse – blaming the people for a decision that lay ultimately at his door. It is ironic that Pontius Pilate is known for two things today. He was the original 'washer of his hands' over a matter for which he felt himself innocent. Yet at the same time he is remembered every Sunday by millions all over the world as the murderer of Jesus:

> …*Crucified under Pontius Pilate*… (From both the Apostles and the Nicene Creed).

No-one is innocent of Christ's blood. Neither the Jews nor the Gentiles, neither the masses nor the rulers. We can perform as many rituals as we like, but we all have blood on our hands.

Yet, amazingly, this is where Christ meets us. You see in the Old Testament tabernacle (and then Temple) there was a basin erected next to the altar. Many times it is commanded that the sacrifices are to be washed before they are slain. Yet in connection with *this* basin, only one kind of washing is commanded. This basin was for the High Priest, to wash his hands (Exodus 30:18f). The one who offers up the sacrifice must show his ceremonial cleanness to the people.

No doubt Pilate was unaware of this detail and yet he fulfilled it publicly. The Lamb of God would be sacrificed according to the law, and the man responsible would wash his hands for all to see. Yet such an act does not vindicate *Pilate*, it vindicates Christ who, though silent like a sheep before its shearers, seems to be pulling the strings in a remarkable way.

For those viewing these events politically, they inspire only cynicism. Pilate is trying to absolve himself, when he should be taking responsibility. For those viewing these events biblically, they inspire deep trust. Even as He suffers the most cosmic miscarriage of justice, Christ remains in control. The condemned Man is convicting the world. The One in the dock is calling the shots. "The Son of man goeth as it is written of Him." (Matthew 26:24). And His *killers* only end up serving His purposes.

Crown of thorns

What does it mean for Jesus to be Redeemer?

What does it mean that He is Saviour of the *world*?

Some people have a gospel that depicts the Son of God swooping down to snatch a lucky few from damnation. *Souls* are saved and saved out of the world into another realm. The world itself can sink into hell – the chosen ones have a life-raft. And they can't wait to escape.

But then Jesus comes into the world and anchors Himself to *this* reality. He earths Himself into our flesh. He takes our humanity to Himself: forever. More than this, He takes our sufferings to Himself – bearing our sorrows and carrying our griefs (Isaiah 53:4). He takes our sins to Himself – the iniquity of us all is laid upon Him at the cross (Isaiah 53:7). And even more than this, He takes our curse upon Himself – lifted up on a tree to bear the reproach we all deserve (Galatians 3:13).

Jesus does not ignore suffering, sin and curse. And He doesn't merely blast it to oblivion with some glory-gun. He takes it to Himself. He owns it and then puts it to death in His own body. The Head of creation dives into this pit of our own making to take on the darkness in person. And there's no better symbol for this than a crown of thorns.

> "The soldiers of the governor took Jesus into the common hall, and gathered unto him the whole band of soldiers. And they stripped him, and put on him a scarlet robe. And when they had platted **a crown of thorns**, they put it upon his head, and a reed in his right hand: and they bowed the knee before him, and mocked him, saying, Hail, King of the Jews!"
> (Matthew 27:27-29)

Thorns are the very emblem of the curse. As soon as Adam sinned the LORD told him:

> "Thorns also and thistles shall [the ground] bring forth to thee."
> (Genesis 3:18)

These thorns are the polar opposite of the fruitfulness for which the earth is intended. And they are the opposite of the fruitfulness God's people are meant for. While Israel is supposed to be a fruitful vine, briers and thorns come up instead (Isaiah 5). Jesus uses the same imagery in His own teaching. When speaking about the false prophets of His day, He asks "Do men gather grapes of thorns?" That is, will you find the life of God in a fraudulent people?

Thorns choke the fruitfulness of the word (Matthew 13:22) and they harm those who are seeking to spread that word (2 Corinthians 12:7). Thorns are anti-life, anti-gospel, anti-creation.

And what does Jesus do? He dives headlong into the thornbush – He enters into the fruitless, lifeless, painful curse of this world. *Through it* there is twisted a crown of thorns, and He wears it with pride.

Christ's reign does not ignore the thorns, it includes them and takes them up into His redemptive purposes. He turns curses into crowns, and a tree intended for death into the very tree of life. Here is a cosmic redemption.

What regrets do you nurse? What sins do you still lament? How many "what ifs" do you wonder about? Have you suffered from foolish, sinful or unfortunate twists of fate? Do you consider that now your life is condemned to God's second, third, fourth or 57th-best? Look again to Christ. He turns curses into crowns. And that's not just an *example* of redemption. The cross is the very engine of redemption. And there is no part of this world that it will not touch.

Whatever thorns you experience, Christ is taking them and twisting them further. He is not discarding them. He's not actually straightening them! He's *twisting* them into a crown. He's pushing on through the curse, through the cross to resurrection blessings. But in these blessings, the curses are not forgotten, they are included. They are glorified. Curses become crowns.

There is no pain, no weakness, no fruitlessness, no sin that Jesus does not take up into His purposes and turn to greater glory. We're not sure *how* He will do it. But when we look at the cross we cannot doubt *that* He will do it. He is the One who turns *deicide* into cosmic glory and blessing. He really is the Redeemer of the world. No matter how painful the thorns might be, we can trust the One who makes them His crown.

30 October – Matthew 27:27-31; Philippians 2:5-11

Hail, King of the Jews!

When you think of a martyr's death, you might picture dignified suffering, noble sacrifice, perhaps a reluctantly admiring crowd, some final, well chosen words of grace and wisdom. We often imagine a certain glory to martyrdom. But that only goes to show we don't know what we're talking about.

Richard Wurmbrand wrote "Tortured for Christ", a stunning, first-person account of the persecution of the Romanian Church under Communist Rule. He remarks at one stage that the most effective way for the government to kill off a pastor is to spread a false rumour among the village that he is a vile sex offender. A mob of local vigilantes would do the rest. Such a man does not die as a hero, he dies as a paedophile – at least in the world's eyes.

Many people imagine an applauding crowd lining the way to martyrdom. But Wurmbrand writes of the reality – those who die for Jesus are rarely known to be dying for Jesus. They are considered the scum of the earth and those who kill them feel entirely justified in ridding the world of their presence. Those put to death are treated as worthy of death. There is no glory, no dignity, no earthly vindication.

But even in this shame, martyrs for Christ share a deep fellowship with their Lord. For His death was the ultimate in shameful degradation. In fact the shame was a key part of His sufferings.

As He looked ahead to His passion, the mockery of the Son of Man was central:

> "And they shall mock him, and shall scourge him, and shall spit upon him, and shall kill him: and the third day he shall rise again." (Mark 10:34)

Jesus will not merely *die* for His creatures. Such sacrifice is astonishing enough. But we could almost imagine Him laying on some altar as fearful and reverent priests shed His blood for the sins of the world. We could picture Him reassuring His hesitant executioners, "Friend, let it be so, I do this for you."

But in reality Jesus stoops infinitely beneath such a death. He's not just murdered but mocked also:

> "Then the soldiers of the governor took Jesus into the common hall, and gathered unto him the whole band of soldiers. And they stripped him, and put on him a scarlet robe. And when they had platted a crown of thorns, they put it upon his head, and a reed in his right hand: and they bowed the knee before him, and mocked him, saying, **Hail, King of the Jews!** And they spit upon him, and took the reed, and smote him on the head. And after that they had mocked him, they took the robe off from him, and put his own raiment on him, and led him away to crucify him."
> (Matthew 27:27-31)

It's an anti-coronation service. In the palace they robe Him, crown Him and proclaim Him King. At the same time they mock Him, spit on Him and punch Him in the face. If this were a mere man it would be shameful. If he were an earthly king it would be treason. But what is it to treat the Lord of Glory like this?

What kind of Lord subjects Himself to such treatment? Not just to death – but to *this* kind of death. He doesn't simply die. He is dissected before a hateful crowd. Stripped naked, teased and spat on by His killers. Punched, and punched and punched again.

Here is a God who cares *nothing* for appearances. Here is a God who cares *nothing* for earthly glory. Literally *nothing* is beneath His dignity. There are no depths which He will not plumb in His mission to save.

Therefore this mock worship is intimately tied to a right honouring of Jesus. Not only will these soldiers one day bow before the vindicated Lord Jesus in true worship. Actually it's Christ's willingness to endure such mockery which makes Him worthy of all praise and glory:

> "Let this mind be in you, which was also in Christ Jesus: Who, being in the form of God, thought it not robbery to be equal with God: But made himself of no reputation, and took upon him the form of a servant, and was made in the likeness of men: And being found in fashion as a man, he humbled himself, and became obedient unto death, even the death of the cross. Wherefore God also hath highly exalted him, and given him a name which is above every name: That at the name of Jesus **every knee should bow**, of things in heaven, and things in earth, and things under the earth; And that every tongue should confess that Jesus Christ is Lord, to the glory of God the Father." (Philippians 2:5-11)

31 October – Luke 23:26-43

Father, forgive them; for they know not what they do

On one occasion I spoke with an atheist who made a repeated claim: "Jesus was a hypocrite." No matter how many times I asked him for evidence, he couldn't point to any. Plenty in me. Plenty in himself. Innumerable instances in Christian history. But none in Christ Himself.

That's quite astonishing really. Hypocrisy is almost the defining characteristic of humanity. We cannot bear to be seen for the unrighteous fools we are and so we wear masks, we hide, we act and distract. And our speech is the primary way we do it. The magician, Derren Brown says he performs his tricks through a mixture of "magic, suggestion, psychology, misdirection and showmanship." That's what *we* do with words to try and "pull off" our own performances.

We say one thing but mean/think/do another. Everyone's a hypocrite. Except Jesus.

But that should shock us more than it does. You see no-one had more scope for hypocrisy than Jesus. Because no-one preached the kind of life that Jesus preached. Let's just take five statements from the sermon on the mount:

> Every jot and tittle of the law must be fulfilled
>
> Turn the other cheek
>
> Go the extra mile
>
> Love your enemies
>
> You cannot serve God and Mammon.

Such talk opens Him up to the closest scrutiny. He has set the bar so high, even to the point of saying "Be ye therefore perfect, even as your Father which is in heaven is perfect." (Matthew 5:48)

If *my* opponents were baying for my blood I can imagine a paralysing fear over the scandals they may dig up. But think of the claims which Christ's enemies could hold Him to. The merest flaw would open Him instantly to the charge of hypocrisy. Instead, what do we see? Perfect integrity. Not even His harshest critics could make their charges stick. Here is the one Man in whom life and lip speak the same language.

Perhaps the clearest example of this is in the hour of His death. Christ maintains His integrity even in the furnace of intense suffering:

> "And there were also two other, malefactors, led with him to be put to death. And when they were come to the place, which is called Calvary, there they crucified him, and the malefactors, one on the right hand, and the other on the left. Then said Jesus, **Father, forgive them; for they know not what they do.**" (Luke 23:32-34)

It's the first of His 'last words'. And it's a word of forgiveness. When I bump my head my first thought is of vengeance. When Christ was pierced, He bled mercy. Iron nails are driven through His hands and feet, His body hoisted onto the upright, His bones out of joint, struggling for breath and He prays "Father, forgive." As *He* bore the curse of God, Christ cries for our mercy.

And so the Man who makes the highest demand – "Love your enemies" – obeys it to its darkest depths. He is as good as His word. But His word is not a judgement upon us hypocrites. It's not even a judgement upon Christ-killers! This is what's so astonishing about the righteousness of Christ. It does not make Him less sympathetic to sinners but *more.*

This is *why* He hangs on the cross. His death is not for the good. It's *for* the very people who cause it. And His prayer is answered the next time this crowd gathered publicly – at the feast of Pentecost. Two months later, Peter proclaimed to the Christ-killers the developments that had occurred since Passover:

> "God hath made that same Jesus, whom ye have crucified, both Lord and Christ. Now when they heard this, they were pricked in their heart, and said unto Peter and to the rest of the apostles, Men and brethren, what shall we do? Then Peter said unto them, Repent, and be baptized every one of you in the name of Jesus Christ for the remission of sins, and ye shall receive the gift of the Holy Ghost… they gladly received his word were baptized: and the same day there were added unto them about three thousand souls." (Acts 2:36-41)

It is an incredible answer to Christ's prayer, an incredible response by God to the murder of His Son. He forgives them the killing of His Son and pledges them the gift of His Spirit. What more can God offer?

On the day of Pentecost, Christ-killers came to know the Fatherly love which Jesus called on even in the hell of Calvary. The Father also proves His integrity in fulfilling His gracious word.

The word of Father and Son to hypocrites is not a word of judgement. As the cross proves, at our very worst He offers His very best. If we come to the cross for mercy we too will know Christ's word on our behalf: "Father, forgive." And He will. He's as good as His word.

1 November – Luke 23:44-49; John 19:28-30

Gave up the ghost

– An old car that breaks down for the last time.

– A sports team that knows it can't win.

– A business that finally calls it quits.

In all these situations we'd say they "gave up the ghost."

In the bible, the phrase describes death. Abraham, Isaac and Jacob were all said to have "given up the ghost" when they died. It just means that they breathed their last breath.

In the biblical languages (and in old English), breath, spirit and ghost were all one word. And so for Abraham and others, it was a case of their body returning to dust and their spirit (or 'ghost') returning to God. (Ecclesiastes 12:7).

We're all destined to give up the ghost. Death is "the way of all the earth" (1 Kings 2:2). And the funeral service has a stark reminder:

> "earth to earth, ashes to ashes, dust to dust"

Our spirits animate us for a while, but soon we give up the ghost. And down to the dust we go.

I don't know what you make of that song from the Lion King, "The circle of life"? It's incredibly catchy, but I can't sing it. When I realise that *I* am dust and I'm destined for the dustbin, I don't feel like singing. Especially since the bible argues it's more of a semi-circle really! If life naturally runs its course then we emerge from the cosmic compost heap only to sink back down to the sludge.

Just after Adam sinned the Lord told him:

> "dust thou art, and unto dust shalt thou return." (Genesis 3:19)

That's the kind of life we've inherited from Adam. It's not a life-*cycle*. It's a one-way arrow pointing straight to the grave. And there's no way out.

Our natural life – the life of the flesh – only produces more flesh. We can't generate spiritual life from our own resources. We are perishing and one day we will all "give up the ghost."

So what does the Son of God do when He sees His handiwork perishing? It should never cease to amaze us: He comes to perish too. Even the Word our Maker gives up the ghost. John was there at the cross to see it happen:

> "Jesus said, It is finished: and he bowed his head, and **gave up the ghost**." (John 19:30)

Here is the Lord of Glory going "the way of all the earth." But why should the Author of life subject Himself to death?

Let's hear the 4th century Bishop, Athanasius:

> "For this purpose, then, the… Word of God entered our world. In one sense, indeed, He was not far from it before, for no part of creation had ever been without Him Who, while ever abiding in union with the Father, yet fills all things that are. But now He entered the world in a new way, stooping to our level in His love and Self-revealing to us. He saw the reasonable race, the race of men that, like Himself, expressed the Father's Mind, wasting out of existence, and death reigning over all in corruption. He saw that corruption held us all the closer, because it was the penalty for the Transgression… All this He saw and, pitying our race, moved with compassion for our limitation, unable to endure that death should have the mastery, rather than that His creatures should perish and the work of His Father for us men come to nought, He took to Himself a body, a human body even as our own… because all our bodies were liable to the corruption of death, He surrendered His body to death instead of all, and offered it to the Father. This He did out of sheer love for us, so that in His death all might die, and the law of death thereby be abolished because, having fulfilled in His body that for which it was appointed, it was thereafter voided of its power for men. This He did that He might turn again to incorruption men who had turned back to corruption, and make them alive through death by the appropriation of His body and by the grace of His resurrection. Thus He would make death to disappear from them as utterly as straw from fire."

When Jesus gave up the ghost it wasn't a failure. On the contrary, as our verse declares, His death "finished" death for us all. It was the very accomplishment of His divine mission. More on this next time…

2 November – John 19:17-37

It is finished

"To die is not a problem when a man has accomplished his historic mission." Unfortunately for Leon Trotsky, an icepick cut short his mission to rule Russia. His death represented a failure. But Christ would have us believe that His death was a success. Yet there was absolutely nothing on Good Friday that looked victorious.

> "After this, Jesus knowing that all things were now accomplished, that the scripture might be fulfilled, saith, I thirst. Now there was

> set a vessel full of vinegar: and they filled a spunge with vinegar, and put it upon hyssop, and put it to his mouth. When Jesus therefore had received the vinegar, he said, **It is finished**: and he bowed his head, and gave up the ghost." (John 19:28-30)

Here we have a 33 year old Jew covered in spittle and blood, stripped of His only possession – His cloak, His back pulped from flogging, His limbs pinned to a piece of wood, His body hoisted onto the upright, an accusation of blasphemy and sedition placarded above Him, His followers scattered, crowds hurling abuse, the sky black and heaven silent. And Jesus waits until *this* moment to cry out "I did it!"

That's the meaning of "It is finished." It's a single Greek word that means 'it is covered, it is satisfied, it is paid for.' Archaeologists have found the word stamped across first century bills. When you made that last mortgage repayment to the building society, the final notice would come back with the stamp: 'it's paid for', 'it's covered', 'you've done it!'

And in His final moments Jesus declares His death to be His victory: "It is finished!" Not '*I* am finished'. This is not a cry of defeat. '*It* is finished'. This is about accomplishment. But what exactly is being accomplished?

Well it's an ancient work that was alluded to in the opening chapters of the Bible. In Genesis 2 we read about the conclusion of the creation week. At the end of the sixth day, "God rested." The LORD brought creation to completion, that all might find rest in a true Sabbath.

Of course the fall puts a major spanner in the works. There is no longer any rest to be found in this old creation, only striving and failing. Therefore a new work of God is afoot.

Fast-forward to John chapter 5 and Jesus gives a sign of the new work. He brings new creation life to a lame man. Of course the authorities – guardians of the old order – are incensed that Jesus would "work" on the Sabbath. He replies:

> "My Father worketh hitherto, and I work." (John 5:17)

The Father and Son have not *retired* from world. Since the fall, the Father and Son have been working to redeem the old creation and bring it to its *true* rest.

This is the great work of God. This is the task which must be "finished" – the destruction of the old order, that new life might be raised up. And here on the cross we see it happening. The Son has become flesh. He has taken humanity to Himself and with it, the headship of this old order. He wraps our death, pain, struggle and curse around Himself so that He might put it into the ground like a seed. *Then* the world can be raised up – born again. (John 12:24)

Picture Him there on the cross. He is lifted up as the Head of this old order – shot through with sin, curse and death. He is a figure of disgust, truly summing up the hell of our plight. And now look at the time. It's Friday afternoon – the end of the sixth day. Sabbath is closing in when no-one may work. And just in the nick of time, He shouts "Finished!"

His work *is* to die, to take this creaking world down into death and finish it off once and for all. On the sixth day, He accomplished His mission. On the Sabbath He rests. And on the Sunday, a whole new world begins.

3 November – Matthew 28:1-15

He is not here, for he is risen

Woody Allen is famously fearful of death (of course he maintains he's not afraid, he just 'doesn't want to be there when it happens'). He was once asked, 'Aren't you pleased to know you'll live on in the hearts and minds of those you've touched?' Woody said 'I don't want to live on in hearts and minds, I want to live on in my apartment.' That's what we all want – resurrection. It's exactly what Jesus offers. And yet it's the last thing we expect.

It sounds like madness to even contemplate "living on in my apartment." Sure, living on in memories is reasonable. And living on in some non-physical, spiritual dimension sounds plausible… at a stretch. But living on in immortal, bodily, earthly life? That's the stuff of fairytales surely. Everything in our natural experience works against resurrection hope. Our ordinary lives teach us to believe Monty Python's line: "Life is quite absurd and death's the final word." Life leads to death. That's the trajectory of this world and of Adam its original head. Life and then death.

But Jesus came to reverse the way of Adam. He came to turn the world right-side-up. And therefore it strikes the children of Adam as utterly new and strange. On that first Easter Sunday, the women came to the tomb expecting to pay their last respects to a departed friend. They came to mark an ending. Instead they were witnesses to the one great beginning:

> "In the end of the sabbath, as it began to dawn toward the first day of the week, came Mary Magdalene and the other Mary to see the sepulchre. And, behold, there was a great earthquake: for the

> angel of the Lord descended from heaven, and came and rolled back the stone from the door, and sat upon it. His countenance was like lightning, and his raiment white as snow: And for fear of him the keepers did shake, and became as dead men. And the angel answered and said unto the women, Fear not ye: for I know that ye seek Jesus, which was crucified. **He is not here: for he is risen**, as he said. Come, see the place where the Lord lay." (Matthew 28:1-6)

Imagine an alternative Easter story. Imagine that the women found the body of Jesus, but were startled by the angel who proclaimed: "This is only the *body* of Jesus. Don't worry, the spirit of Jesus lives on, and so will you when you die. Don't be afraid, you will meet with Jesus again when you've all gotten rid of your earthly encumbrances." What kind of gospel would that be? The Apostle Paul answered in 1 Corinthians 15:

> "And if Christ be not risen, then is our preaching vain, and your faith is also vain…. if Christ be not raised, your faith is vain; ye are yet in your sins. Then they also which are fallen asleep in Christ are perished. If in this life only we have hope in Christ, we are of all men most miserable." (1 Corinthians 15:14-19)

Some sort of life beyond death is not good news. The gospel of God is that Christ has entered His own world to remake it from the inside. He has come as our true Head, to take hold of the old world and put it down to the death it deserves. The old order *is* a matter of 'life unto death', and that's where Jesus takes it. But then He rises up again to reverse the way of all flesh.

That's why it's so critical that He rises with the same body. He is not abandoning Creation 1.0 and starting 2.0. He is recapitulating His handiwork – going over the old ground and redeeming it all. He is risen in *that same body* because He wills to fix *this very world.* And just as the old body is restored and glorified, so will the whole universe.

On that first *day* of the week a new beginning was birthed. Jesus had put the old to death on the 6th day. He'd rested on the Sabbath, and brought light and immortality to life on the first day. Jesus renews all things by rising up as the true and better Adam, the eternal King. And as surely as the King was raised – so His Kingdom will also be raised. Therefore "fear not"!

Doubting Thomas

"If God came down right now, I'd believe. If He showed up in all His Godness and proved Himself to me, I'd bow down and worship. I won't believe if I can't see, hear and touch Him – but if He appears, I'll believe."

Have you ever said that? Or thought it? Well, that's Thomas' question.

> "Except I shall see in his hands the print of the nails, and put my finger into the print of the nails, and thrust my hand into his side, I will not believe." (John 20:25)

Thomas wasn't there when Jesus had appeared to the other disciples the week before. And he doesn't believe the eye-witness testimony of the apostles. He wants his own proof. Tangible, in your face, see it, touch it, taste it, feel it, proof.

But he is knocked off his feet when this proof comes. Verse 26:

> "And after eight days again his disciples were within, and Thomas with them: then came Jesus, the doors being shut, and stood in the midst, and said, Peace be unto you. Then saith he to Thomas, Reach hither thy finger, and behold my hands; and reach hither thy hand, and thrust it into my side: and be not faithless, but believing." (John 20:26-27)

Thomas had wanted to see these wounds. He *demanded* to see these wounds. And so Jesus gives him more than he bargained for. He even invites Thomas to *thrust his hand into His side!* Incredible.

Jesus seems proud of His scars. He displays them as badges of honour, because these wounds carry a scar story that beats every scar story ever told.

All scar stories have a certain shape: *I was travelling along quite nicely until I encountered… a dog / a ball / a car / a fist / the force of gravity. It hurt a lot, but I'm ok now. And I have the scars to prove it.*

Jesus' scar story goes something like this: *Things were fine until I encountered… planet earth. They did their worst to me, and it hurt immensely. But I'm ok now. And I have the scars to prove it.*

So there is Jesus confronting Thomas with His war wounds – the marks of His suffering love. And in verse 28 Thomas can't control himself any more: He exclaims to Jesus, "My LORD and my God."

It's one of the mountaintop declarations of the Bible. And what has prompted it? The *wounds* of Jesus. This is not a cowering response to the *strength* of Christ's resurrection. This is worship elicited by the sacrificial *love* of His death. Thomas understands the scar story. He sees that Jesus has come to our aid and stuck up for us in the only fight that really matters. And He's won. In gratitude and praise, Thomas cries out "My LORD and my God."

Not simply, "*The* LORD" but "*my* LORD". It's personal.

Is it personal for you? Or are you still something of a doubting Thomas?

But perhaps you're thinking, "It's alright for Thomas. He got to *see* Jesus. What about me?"

That's why Jesus answers with verse 29:

> "Jesus saith unto him, Thomas, because thou hast seen me, thou hast believed: blessed are they that have not seen, and yet have believed."

Blessed are people when they are *not like Thomas*. Blessed are we when we *don't* see and yet believe. How is that possible? John's Gospel continues:

> "And many other signs truly did Jesus in the presence of his disciples, which are not written in this book: ***But these are written, that ye might believe*** that Jesus is the Christ, the Son of God; and that believing ye might have life through his name." (John 20:30-31)

We can have a more blessed experience than Thomas. How? We can trust the written, eye-witness testimony. And Jesus says that these Scriptures (of which John's Gospel is a part) are better than a one-off resurrection experience.

How could that be true? Well just imagine that Jesus appeared to you tonight at the end of your bed. Imagine you saw His wounds and heard Him say 'Peace' to you personally. That would give you a spiritual high for days. Weeks, even!

But fairly soon you'd start to wonder whether you'd dreamt the whole thing. People would ridicule you for your claims and pretty soon you'd need another appearance.

If you have ever asked for an extraordinary appearance of God, you are asking for something that will impress you today but will ultimately make you doubt more than believe.

It is more blessed – it is better – to go on the eye-witness testimony of the Bible. Because with the Bible, it's there in black and white for all time. At three in the morning when I have doubts. When loved ones die. When I've lost my job. I can always see Jesus, by opening my Bible and seeing Him in the sacred story.

If I had physically touched the risen Christ twelve years ago – by now my memory would have faded. Instead I met Jesus in the pages of the Bible, and I am seeing Him ***more*** clearly today than when I first believed. As I go deeper into the Bible His wounds are more vivid, His scar story is more real, His love seems more profound – all through the pages of Scripture.

All of us are a Doubting Thomas at various times and to various degrees. But the Holy Spirit has given us an antidote:

> "These are written, that ye might believe."

If that's true – how should we read our Bibles? Answer: Expectantly. We should seek a more blessed encounter than the Upper Room. We should desire a coming of Christ, a sight of His war wounds and response of worship – "My LORD and my God."

5 November – Matthew 28:16-20

In the name of the Father and of the Son and of the Holy Spirit

Thomas Jefferson once wrote:

> "When we shall have done away the incomprehensible jargon of the Trinitarian arithmetic, that three are one, and one is three; when we shall have knocked down the artificial scaffolding, reared to mask from view the simple structure of Jesus; when, in short, we shall have unlearned everything which has been taught since His day, and got back to the pure and simple doctrines He inculcated, we shall then be truly and worthily His disciples."

Jefferson is not alone. Many *Christians* consider the Trinity to be a mathematical problem, an artificial scaffolding and an obscurity that masks the simple teaching of Jesus. Yet to think this way is to *deny* the very Person and teaching of Jesus.

Trinity and the Person of Jesus

It denies the *Person* of Jesus because He *is*, most fundamentally, "the Christ, the Son of God." Both Mark's Gospel and John's Gospel are structured around that full name of Jesus – "the Christ, the Son of God." This means that He is the One anointed (Christed) without measure by the Spirit and the One eternally begotten of the Father. To know Jesus is to be introduced to His Spirit and His Father. In short, to understand Jesus is *already* to be drawn into a knowledge of the Three Persons. And to know the Spirit and Father *in* the Son, is to know the Three as Persons united together in love.

This *is* the doctrine of the Trinity: God is three Persons united in love. There is no mathematical conundrum here. It's clear how God is Three – there are Three distinct Persons. It's also clear how God is One – the Three Persons are united in love. That's how one-ness happens in the Bible. Adam and Eve are *one* because they are united in love. The Church is meant to be *one* by being united in love (John 17:21-22). And the Father, Son and Spirit are one through love. In fact they are *so* one that they *cannot* be without each other. The Father is Father *of* the Son – without whom He would cease to be who He is. Likewise, the Son is Son *of* the Father – without whom He would cease to be who He is, etc, etc.

The Three are so much *One* that they are '*in*' one another. This loving, mutual in-dwelling *is* the unity of the three. And that's where we get the word "trinity" from. It's the "tri-unity" – the loving unity of the three. This is who our God is.

Trinity and the Teaching of Jesus

Not only is the Trinity simply the explication of the Person of Jesus. Contrary to Jefferson's assertion, the Trinity is the *teaching* of Jesus too.

Just before He ascended to heaven, He commanded His disciples:

> "Go ye therefore, and teach all nations, baptizing them **in the name of the Father, and of the Son, and of the Holy Ghost**." (Matthew 28:19)

Notice that there are not three names here. There is only one name – but that one name is constituted by these three Persons – the Father, Son and Holy Ghost.

What we have here is, essentially, the Aaronic blessing brought into the New Testament. In Numbers 6, the High Priest was meant to put the *name* of God onto the people. And that name involved three different divine movements:

> "Speak unto Aaron and unto his sons, saying, On this wise ye shall bless the children of Israel, saying unto them, The LORD bless thee, and keep thee: The LORD make his face shine upon

> thee, and be gracious unto thee: The LORD lift up his countenance upon thee, and give thee peace. And they shall put my name upon the children of Israel; and I will bless them." (Numbers 6:23-27)

The first movement is blessing and keeping. The second movement is the revelation of God's radiant Face to shine in grace. The third movement is turning that light personally upon the people to give them peace.

And now Jesus tells His followers – *You are all priestly. But now it's a priesthood to the nations. Bring them in and put God's name on them. The Father is the Fountain of all blessing. The Son is the shining Face, radiating God's grace. The Spirit turns the world to that Radiance to give them peace.*

When we put these truths together, what do we have?

Well a disciple of 'the Christ, the Son of God' is filled with His Spirit and adopted by His Father. Such a person is a little christ, a little son or daughter of God. And the sign of this reality is baptism into the Triune Name where a person is brought into the sphere of the Triune blessing. Here the Spirit ever turns us to the Son, in whose face we see the Source of all blessing, the Glorious Father.

The Trinity is not incomprehensible arithmetic. "The Father, Son and Holy Ghost" is not a problem to be solved. The Trinity is the very name and nature of God. And in the loving unity of Father, Son and Holy Spirit, we find our place – united to Jesus, anointed with the Spirit and calling on our Abba, Father.

Jefferson could not be more wrong. The Trinity is not the scaffolding – it is the very centre of our faith. There is nothing purer, simpler or more worthy in all the doctrines of Christ!

6 November – Acts 2:1-41

The fruit of his loins

If this phrase is used today it's usually as a playful archaism.

> – "That's my boy," says the teasing father, "the fruit of my loins."
>
> – "Dad!!!"

But actually it's a great compliment. There's only one person in the Bible who is specifically referred to as 'loin-fruit': Jesus. Well of course – the One who is the original Seed, comes in the fullness of time as Fruit.

Let's get the context for this phrase.

It's the day of Pentecost. 50 days since Jesus rose from the dead. 10 days since He ascended into heaven. And on this Sunday, the Holy Spirit comes in power to clothe the church for its witness to the world.

At the time, the whole nation of Israel was gathered to celebrate the ancient festival of Pentecost. It's seven weeks after that post-Passover festival of "Firstfruits" when the green shoots of the coming harvest were presented to God. Now at Pentecost, the new batch of grain is brought before the LORD (Leviticus 23:15-21). It isn't just firstfruits, this is now the harvest, and everyone would be thinking of "fruit."

Now remember the last time these Israelites were all together. It was Passover when they had cried out unanimously: "Crucify Him, Crucify Him!" And in spite of their hatred, the Lord Jesus responded on the cross: "Father, forgive." Now, as the Christ-killers reconvene, there's an opportunity for Christ's prayer to be answered.

The Holy Spirit empowers the disciples to speak to the international gathering – each one hearing them in their native language. It's a wonderful miracle for Pentecost, breaking down barriers so that all sorts of "new grain" might be harvested. Peter steps forward to explain this sign of new life coming upon the world (Acts 2). First he quotes Joel and explains how the ancient prophet predicted this breakdown of the old barriers. The end times are now upon us, just as the Scriptures foresaw.

From verse 22-32 Peter narrates the events of Christ's life as the fulfillment of another prophet. According to Peter, David was a prophet and knew "that God had sworn with an oath to him, that of **the fruit of his loins**, according to the flesh, he would raise up Christ to sit on his throne; He seeing this before spake of the resurrection of Christ." (Acts 2:30-31)

The Psalms are not ultimately chronicling David's *own* experiences of suffering and glory. King David knowingly put words to the experiences of the Messiah – who would be the fruit of his loins. David looked forward to his Seed who would be planted into the ground but raised up by God to be a fruitful Vine for all.

People commonly talk of living on in their progeny. David was someone who really could trust in that! That's because Christ, his Seed, was the Firstfruits of a bumper crop of resurrection.

Here is the true meaning of Pentecost. At Passover the Seed died. On the third day, He rose again – the Firstfruits of those who have fallen asleep (1 Corinthians 15:20). And on the basis of this Firstfruits, the world can be grafted in to find new life where before there was only death and barrenness. The Fruit of David's loins was not only fruitful for Himself, He has enough life bursting out of Him for a cosmic harvest.

7 November – Acts 2:36-47

Cut to the heart

When we're "cut to the heart" it's usually because we've been insulted or betrayed or broken up with.

But three times in the book of Acts, the Israelites are "cut" or "pricked" to the heart (Acts 2:37; 5:33; 7:54). Yet with them it's different. Here's what pricks their hearts: the preaching of the Apostles. As the *sins* of the Israelites are uncovered so it feels like a dagger in their chest.

Let's examine the first instance of hearts *pricked* by the gospel…

The Duchess of Cambridge was bullied terribly at school. Though nobody knew it at the time.

While Kate Middleton was at Downe House school she was bullied so badly that her parents took her out after just two terms.

I wonder what those bullies think now?

Maybe the last time they saw her up close they had reduced her to tears. Maybe they laughed and cheered and said good riddance when Kate finally left. Maybe they thought that nothing would ever come of the most unpopular girl in school.

How wrong they were! Through her Prince, she's now royalty. And one day she will be Queen over those bullies! I'm guessing that her old classmates have changed their mind about Kate Middleton.

Acts 2 speaks of a similar but vastly more significant change of mind. Peter is addressing the crowd that, 7 weeks earlier, had bayed for Jesus' blood. Peter, full of the Holy Spirit, pulls no punches:

> "Therefore let all the house of Israel know assuredly, that God hath made that same Jesus, whom ye have crucified, both Lord and Christ." (Acts 2:36)

The charge here is nothing short of deicide – the murder of God Himself! You see, they might have thought little of Jesus in the days of His flesh, but in resurrection God has declared the truth about Jesus: He is Lord and Christ. How would you feel if you were in the crowd?

If you had bullied someone at school, and it turned out they were the son of the headmaster, you would be worried.

What if you'd bullied the Son of *God*, how much trouble do you think you'd be in?

What if you'd *killed* the Son of God, what then?

Peter says "You crucified the LORD of Glory."

How do you respond to such a message? Here's what the people do. Verse 37:

> "Now when they heard this, they were **pricked in their heart**, and said unto Peter and to the rest of the apostles, Men and brethren, what shall we do?"

Pricked in the heart. Peter's words are like a sword straight through them. What should they do?

Should they try to run and hide? Where would they hide? God's quite good at hide and seek. He usually wins that one.

Should they hope that God forgets? He's not particularly absent minded, God.

Should they try to make it up to God? How could they make it up to God? They haven't just stolen stationery from the workplace – they've killed the Lord of Glory!

What should they do? What could they do? Surely this is *it* for these bullies, these murderers. What hope could there be? Well Peter gives some incredibly good news:

> "Then Peter said unto them, Repent, and be baptized every one of you in the name of Jesus Christ for the remission of sins, and ye shall receive the gift of the Holy Ghost." (Acts 2:38)

This is unprecedented grace. Peter says that God wants to forgive the killers of His Son. And not just forgive them, He wants to give them a gift.

Have you ever heard of a Judge who says "I know you're guilty but I forgive you." Can you imagine a Judge whose *son* was murdered saying "I know you're guilty but I forgive you"? Can you imagine a Judge whose son was murdered saying, "I know you're guilty, but I forgive you *and* I want to give you a gift." And imagine he says "Here's my gift – have my daughter's hand in marriage!" Unthinkable. But that's just what God is like. He wants to forgive us and give us a gift – the gift of His Spirit. Another Family Member if you like.

He gives us One Family Member – His Son. We kill Him and He pays us back by giving us His Other Family Member, His Spirit! That's *everything* He has to give us. It's incomparable grace. And in the light of it, Peter implores them to change their mind.

That's what repent means: change your mind. Jesus is Lord. He is the Christ.

It's like with Kate Middleton. Those bullies used to call her Flaky Pimpletongue. Now she's the Duchess of Cambridge. One day they will call her Queen. I imagine those bullies have changed their mind about Kate. But the world needs to do the same with Jesus. We used to think He was an inconvenience. We used to try to silence Him. Perhaps we used to use Jesus' name as a swear word. At best we used to think of Him as a mere teacher or example. We were wrong. He is Lord and Christ and raised to God's right hand to rule the world. So repent – change your mind… and be baptised.

You see, Jesus was baptized into our kind of life – He stood in our shoes to do life in our place. Now, says Peter, you should get baptised into *Him.* Be clothed in Him – in His kind of life.

United to Jesus, the gift of the Holy Spirit is freely offered as well as the remission of all our sins. It's the most incredible promise. Who's it for? Surely it's for good people, religious people, respectable people, the super-keen? No, says Peter. Verse 39 – this promise is for *you.* The promise is for Christ-killers!

For the promise is unto you, and to your children, and to all that are afar off, even as many as the Lord our God shall call.

You can't be too bad, you can't be too immature, you can't be too far from God – the promise is for you. Because Christ is for you. He's even for His killers. He is most definitely for you.

In spite of the worst crimes imaginable we are given God's Son, we are given His Spirit, we are forgiven all our sins and called home to God's Family Life. All we've ever done is cause His death. All He's ever done is give us *more.* When we see this gospel reality, our heart are not just pricked, they are melted.

8 November – Acts 9:1-31

Damascus Road Experience

It's shorthand for any dramatic conversion. People have often said to me that they're Christians but they're still waiting for their "Damascus Road Experience."

But they will have to wait for Christ's return for anything like what Paul experienced. You see the Damascus Road was not just the conversion of a man, it was the creation of an Apostle. And Apostles needed to have met the risen Christ – both the 11 and Paul himself acknowledge that (Acts 1:21-22; 1 Corinthians 15:1-11). Therefore something extraordinary was needed to turn Saul of Tarsus into Paul the Apostle. The risen Christ had to personally appear. But He didn't *have* to appear to a man like Saul! This conversion would model the sheer grace of the Lord.

For a start, Saul was a Pharisee. He describes his past like this:

> "Circumcised the eighth day, of the stock of Israel, of the tribe of Benjamin, an Hebrew of the Hebrews; as touching the law, a Pharisee;" (Philippians 3:5)

When Jesus chose the original twelve he chose a tax-collector, Matthew. He also chose a Zealot, Simon. These two were hated and feared members of the establishment and anti-establishment respectively. Nonetheless, there was place in Christ's kingdom for all manner of publicans *and* sinners. Yet all the while the Pharisees remained firmly on the outside, muttering (Luke 15:1-2).

Now Christ steps in with compelling force and claims a Pharisee for His own. And not just any Pharisee – the chief persecutor of the early church. Saul oversaw the killing of Stephen in Acts 7 and was known to believers everywhere as "he that destroyed" Christians. (Acts 9:21)

So how was Saul prepared for this religious experience? Was he particularly soft-hearted and receptive to the grace of Jesus that day? No. The grace of Jesus is not *attracted* to soft-heartedness, the grace of Jesus creates soft-heartedness where before there was stony opposition. Here is the context of Saul's conversion:

> "And Saul, yet breathing out threatenings and slaughter against the disciples of the Lord, went unto the high priest, And desired of him letters to Damascus to the synagogues, that if he found any of this way, whether they were men or women, he might bring them bound unto Jerusalem. And as he journeyed, he came near Damascus: and suddenly there shined round about him a light from heaven: And he fell to the earth, and heard a voice saying unto him, Saul, Saul, why persecutest thou me? And he

> said, Who art thou, Lord? And the Lord said, I am Jesus whom thou persecutest: it is hard for thee to kick against the pricks." (Acts 9:1-5)

Saul is not *ready* for Jesus. Saul is breathing out slaughter against Christ and His people. And notice how personally Jesus takes it. According to Jesus, Saul has been persecuting Himself. The risen Christ is not above and beyond the struggles of this world. He feels His people's suffering keenly. He is the Head and His body is hurting – therefore Christ Himself is hurting.

Persecuted Christians need to know this. Christ feels this pain and knows how to confront the perpetrators, in His own time and in His own way. But be prepared for Christ to approach the wrong-doers with mercy. This is how He comes to Saul. He even pities his enemy: "It is hard for thee to kick against the pricks." "Pricks" are the sharp goads at the end of a shepherd's crook. Sheep going astray harm themselves on the sharpened points and then harm themselves further by kicking against them. That has been Saul's life. Brought up in the Scriptures, confronted by Christ on every page yet twisting and turning from Him at every opportunity. Conversion for Saul means the end of that kind of suffering. But it will mean a very different kind of suffering from now on.

You see he is blinded by his vision and healed by a Christian called Ananias. Ananias is told by the Lord:

> "[Paul] is a chosen vessel unto me, to bear my name before the Gentiles, and kings, and the children of Israel: For I will shew him how great things he must suffer for my name's sake." (Acts 9:15-16)

Saul is converted from one kind of suffering – a swimming against the stream of his existence – to another kind of suffering – a swimming against the stream of the world. We can go with the world's flow and run up against the Lord, or we can walk with the Lord and go against the world's flow. Paul is summoned to live for Christ's name's sake.

And here is the effect. Jesus says to him:

> "But rise, and stand upon thy feet: for I have appeared unto thee for this purpose, to make thee a minister and a witness both of these things which thou hast seen, and of those things in the which I will appear unto thee; Delivering thee from the people, and from the Gentiles, unto whom now I send thee, To open their eyes, and to turn them from darkness to light, and from the power of Satan unto God, that they may receive forgiveness of

> sins, and inheritance among them which are sanctified by faith that is in me." (Acts 26:15-18)

This is exactly what happens. Paul goes on to live one of the most influential lives the world has ever seen. He writes half of the New Testament and plants churches all around the eastern half of the Mediterranean. Thus the church's greatest enemy is converted to its greatest asset. That's what the grace of God does – turns calamity into even greater blessing. And it does so not because of any goodness in us, but despite our deepest evil. You see the witness of Paul to the grace of Jesus is not diminished by his terrible past, but magnified by it. This murderous blasphemer is able to say:

> "This is a faithful saying, and worthy of all acceptation, that Christ Jesus came into the world to save sinners; of whom I am chief." (1 Timothy 1:15)

The conversion of Paul is not meant to make us despair – as though we could never experience such a change. The conversion of Paul gives us hope. The grace of Jesus extends even to His greatest enemies. It most definitely extends to me.

9 November – Acts 17:1-15

Turned the world upside down

On Good Friday, Christianity was "down and out." The Christ was dead and buried. His followers were despondent and scattered. And that should have been that.

Yet, within a very short period of time, Christ's people were said to be 'turning the world upside down.' How did such an extraordinary revolution happen? Not through the sword, not through political machinations, not even through grass-roots activism. The world was turned upside-down in the first century (and continues to be turned upside-down today) through the preaching of a message.

Just look at the context for this phrase… In Acts 17 Paul and his associates go to the Greek city of Thessalonica.

> "And Paul, as his manner was, went in unto them [at the synagogue], and three sabbath days reasoned with them out of the scriptures, Opening and alleging, that Christ must needs have suffered, and risen again from the dead; and that this Jesus, whom I preach unto you, is Christ." (Acts 17:2-3)

Here's what was so volatile – the preaching of a 'reasoned', 'scriptural' *message*. The message concerns a King – the Christ. But this King is unlike all our expectations for kings. He suffers and dies before rising again. Yet it's this upside-down message that unleashes an upside-down revolution.

You see some Thessalonians believed Paul's message. The Jews that didn't, 'moved with envy', stirred up trouble for the apostles. And this was their report to the powers that be:

> "These that have **turned the world upside down** are come hither also." (Acts 17:7)

Perhaps we think it's counter-intuitive that a *message* "turns the world upside down." But let's consider the impact of this message over the last 20 centuries in the areas of politics, science and economics. The gospel of the suffering and rising Christ has made all the difference…

When people believe that the Lord of all became a servant (or, as Mark 10:45 calls Him, "a minister") then our understanding of earthly power is transformed. The most powerful needs to be the prime *minister* – the chief servant.

When people believe that the Ruler of heaven reigns *as* Man and even *because* He is now Man, then we start to believe that government should be "of the people, for the people and by the people."

When people believe that the Logic of all creation took flesh (John 1:14) and was seen, handled, tested and known (1 John 1:1-4), then we start to study the world in a new way. The Word who became flesh leads us to expect *both* Laws *and* empirical testing to discover those laws. If we only believe in "laws" we will create philosophers. If we only believe in "empirical testing" we will create technology. But for the modern scientific method you need both. Without the Biblical worldview it is inconceivable that science as we know it could have arisen.

When people believe that God's riches – His grace – should not be paid back to God (as though He needs anything) but freely paid forwards to our fellow man, then we begin having a different view of earthly riches. Freed by God's grace we stop hoarding or displaying our wealth and start paying it forwards, re-investing it. And we begin to realise the truth of Christ's words "freely you have received, freely give."

These are just some of the macro-effects of the gospel message on our culture. None of them are, strictly, part of the message. They are simply outworkings of the gospel in a culture where this message is taken seriously. In addition to these fringe benefits, people are brought to an intimate knowledge of the living God, set free from the powers that enslave them, cleansed from guilt and shame, and given the status, power and indeed *life* of Christ. What's more, in Christ they are bonded together into a community of grace – witnesses in the world to God's reconciling love. They are salt and light and the world cannot help but be changed.

What changes the world? Not our doings, but the proclamation of *His* doing. That's the power to turn the world upside down.

10 October – Acts 17:16-34

In Him we live and move and have our being

How do we proclaim the gospel to a world that thinks so differently?

"Contextualisation" is a buzz word in some Christian circles to describe the way our message needs to be fitted to our surroundings. Today's phrase is often used as a prime example of how Paul drew on the truths already present in the culture to build up a credible gospel presentation. You see "In Him we live and move and have our being" was originally a line from an ancient Greek poet. Yet Paul uses the phrase to further his gospel proclamation.

So how do we relate the gospel word to an unbelieving world?

Well last time we learnt the truth that the Christian message "turns the world upside-down". It is the subversion of all our natural thinking. Therefore when this message meets the philosophers of Athens, we expect to see quite a clash. Which is exactly how Acts 17 continues…

> "Now while Paul waited for [Silas and Timothy] at Athens, his spirit was stirred in him, when he saw the city wholly given to idolatry. Therefore disputed he in the synagogue with the Jews, and with the devout persons, and in the market daily with them that met with him. Then certain philosophers of the Epicureans, and of the Stoicks, encountered him. And some said, What will this babbler say? other some, He seemeth to be a setter forth of strange gods: because he preached unto them Jesus, and the resurrection." (Acts 17:16-18)

Other visitors to Athens may have marvelled at the temples and statues, Paul was incensed. He did not see these other gods as stepping stones to Jesus but as idols, pure and simple. In contrast, Paul proclaimed "strange gods." In fact the Athenians seem to have thought that Paul was preaching two gods: Jesus and Anastasia (the Greek for 'resurrection')! Paul was not seeking common ground on the basis of 'some notion of deity', he dives straight in with the Lord Jesus and His resurrection. And this, in spite of the unpopularity of "resurrection" to the Greek mind (v32!). It all just seemed like so much "babble" to the cultured Athenians.

But why? We know that Paul was a wonderful communicator, millions still read his letters. We know that these philosophers were experienced at comprehending new ideas (v21), yet the gospel sounds to them like 'gobble-di-gook'. Paul would explain it in 1 Corinthians:

> "The preaching of the cross is, to them that perish, foolishness." (1 Corinthians 1:18)

Yet Paul persists (as should we all). And when he has another opportunity, he sets out his message once again.

> "Then Paul stood in the midst of Mars' hill, and said, Ye men of Athens, I perceive that in all things ye are too superstitious. For as I passed by, and beheld your devotions, I found an altar with this inscription, TO THE UNKNOWN GOD. Whom therefore ye ignorantly worship, him declare I unto you." (Acts 17:22-23)

Some see this opening as Paul's establishment of common ground. Yet if there's anything which Paul concedes to the Athenians it is their ignorance. The one thing they seem to know is that they don't know God. But Paul will simply declare Him:

> "God that made the world and all things therein, seeing that he is Lord of heaven and earth, dwelleth not in temples made with hands; Neither is worshipped with men's hands, as though he needed any thing, seeing he giveth to all life, and breath, and all things;" (Acts 17:24-25)

We don't make houses for the gods, God makes a home for us. We don't serve Him, He serves us. He doesn't need us, we need Him. It's all so blatantly obvious, and yet the very foundations of human religion are founded on folly. And it's folly which Paul is keen to point out.

He continues by presenting the Gospel of the Two Men. This is something he also does in Romans 5 and 1 Corinthians 15. He tells the story of the world as the story of Adam and Christ. First he tells us of the original man, from whom all nations of men have come…

> "And hath made of one blood all nations of men for to dwell on all the face of the earth, and hath determined the times before appointed, and the bounds of their habitation; That they should seek the Lord, if haply they might feel after him, and find him, though he be not far from every one of us: **For in him we live, and move, and have our being**; as certain also of your own poets have said, For we are also his offspring. Forasmuch then as

> we are the offspring of God, we ought not to think that the Godhead is like unto gold, or silver, or stone, graven by art and man's device." (Acts 17:26-29)

In verse 28 Paul quotes from Epimenides (the original source of today's saying) and from Phaenomena. It's the equivalent of a preacher citing the latest pop song. Of course he uses these Greek quotes to speak *against* Greek culture. He's saying "If you really believed what you sing about, how could you live how you live?" Paul is not vindicating the latent wisdom of the Greeks, he is exposing their foolish inconsistencies. Epimenides spoke far better than he knew and far better than the Greeks lived. On the *preacher's* lips the truth is commandeered and pressed into gospel service. Yet on the poet's lips it stands only to reveal their folly. But such folly must end…

> "The times of this ignorance God winked at; but now commandeth all men every where to repent: Because he hath appointed a day, in the which he will judge the world in righteousness by that man whom he hath ordained; whereof he hath given assurance unto all men, in that he hath raised him from the dead." (Acts 17:30-31)

Here is the second man in Paul's sermon. The Man Jesus Christ answers the man Adam. Jesus passed through the door marked 'death' – the door through which we all must pass – and He came out the other side. When we pass through that door we are assured that *He* is the One to meet us.

He is the Judge. Therefore we must repent. We must completely change our thinking – that's how Paul unpacks the meaning of "repentance." Our minds must be reconfigured by this gospel story.

The gospel does not confront us as one truth among many. It sets a question mark over all 'truths'. It does not build on our nascent religious or philosophical intuitions, it supplants them. In short, it shows us what should be so obvious and yet it strikes the fallen mind as revolutionary – God does not live in the intellectual worlds that we build for Him. No – we live in *His* world. For in Him we live and move and have our being.

11 November – Acts 20:13-38

It is more blessed to give than to receive

Jesus' version of it is probably the most famous – but *everyone* says "it's better to give than receive." All the religions say it. Even the atheists say it.

Last year, UCLA life scientists released a study showing the health benefits of providing support to others. There are many such studies around. They generally find that altruistic behaviour is beneficial, not simply for the recipient but for the giver.

Why might that be? Well evolutionary psychologists proffer explanations like "reciprocal altruism" – when we perform a good deed we might reasonably expect them to return the favour. Simply our anticipation of their pay-back feels good.

Evolutionary psychology, for all of its fascinating findings, reminds me of that old adage: "If all you've got is a hammer, everything looks like a nail." Basic selfishness is a brilliant explanation for so much of human life. But it doesn't capture everything, and trying to make it capture everything leads to unconvincing explanations, like this one.

If "reciprocal altruism" explained our "blessedness" in giving, Jesus should have said "It is more blessed to *receive* than to give, but, hey, giving's a great way of getting!"

Or how about this for an explanation. One of the UCLA scientists said:

> "Because of the importance of support-giving for the survival of our species, it is possible that over the course of our evolutionary history, support-giving may have become psychologically rewarding to ensure that this behaviour persisted."

If this were the case, Jesus should have said "It is more blessed to receive than to give, but remember to factor in the survival of the species over several millenia when you make your self-interested calculations."

Once again, we've avoided the blessedness of *true* self-giving. Self-giving is affirmed close-up, but denied when we zoom back to get the big picture.

Yet in Acts 20:35 Paul recounts a saying of Jesus that was not recorded by the four Evangelists but which was clearly remembered and circulated by the early church: "It is more blessed to give than to receive."

Such a sentiment is expressed in virtually every other world-view imaginable. There's only one difference with Christ's saying… the Speaker. You see "Evolutionary Psychology" may tell you it's better to give, but Evolution itself is selfishness writ large. Other gods may urge you to be selfless – but they themselves are self-interested *takers*. The difference with Christ's saying is Christ.

He *is* ultimate reality and He Himself is self-giving love, the cross proves it. The universe with Christ at the centre is the one universe in which grace reigns. He is the one Lord who does not come to be served but to serve and to give His life for us (Mark 10:45).

There are many exemplars of self-giving, but they operate contrary to the selfish universe they claim to inhabit. There are many that claim to be ultimate powers who tell you to give – but these powers are themselves self-interested. Christ is the one Power who a) tells you to give, b) *is* Giver and c) determines ultimate reality. Jesus tells you to give because He *is* grace poured out beyond all limits. And because *the Lord* is grace, so self-giving is not a means towards ultimate selfishness. Grace is the essence of the blessed life. There's nothing higher, or deeper, or more real. This is *Christ's* universe. So give.

12 November – Romans 1:1-17; Colossians 1:15-23

Saints

"You're a saint!" they exclaim. And it feels nice to be called that. Though obviously we bat away the compliment. Because we know it's mock praise for a minor act of kindness. We know they don't *really* think of us as a saint. You see in most people's understanding *saints* are unapproachable, austere and long-dead individuals. They're not *real people*, not *down-to-earth folk*.

But the Apostle Paul thought of saints very differently. When he wrote his letters to the churches he commonly called whole congregations "saints" (Romans, 1 Corinthians, 2 Corinthians, Ephesians, Philippians and Colossians).

> "To all that be in Rome, beloved of God, called *to be* **saints**: Grace to you and peace from God our Father, and the Lord Jesus Christ." (Romans 1:7)

The italics you can see in this verse are original to the KJV. They convey that the translators have added words which are not based on any underlying Greek words. They have supplied the verb "to be" here, even though there is no such verb in Paul's original statement. More literally Paul says that the Romans are "called saints." That is their status. That is a declaration that stands over them. God calls them saints – not in the future but right now.

See how Paul puts it more straightforwardly in Ephesians:

> "Paul, an apostle of Jesus Christ by the will of God, to the saints which are at Ephesus." (Ephesians 1:1)

Here were ordinary Christians, some of them well-bred, but most of them not (1 Corinthians 1:26). Some of them cultured, some of them not (Romans 1:14). Some of them Jews, some of them Gentiles (Romans 1:16). All of them were sinners (Romans 3:23). Nonetheless, all of them, through faith in Jesus, are called "saints." And we, if we have trusted Christ, can call ourselves "saints." I'm well within my rights to introduce myself as "St Glen." My business card can read "Glen Scrivener: Saint." And so can yours if you're a Christian.

But what does it mean? Well the word literally means "holy ones." Saints are special ones, devoted ones, set apart ones. And yet, there's nothing in our natural circumstance that would warrant the label. There's nothing in our genes, nothing in our grooming, nothing even in our behaviour that makes us saintly. But, here is the central message of Saint Paul: unholy ones like you and me are declared to be holy, not because of our saintly deeds, but purely through the work of the Holy One, Jesus. As Paul says in his letter to the Colossians:

> "And you, that were sometime alienated and enemies in your mind by wicked works, yet now hath he reconciled in the body of his flesh through death, to present you holy and unblameable and unreproveable in his sight." (Colossians 1:21-22)

Let me ask you a question: How does God see you?

We tend to think the answer to that lies on a sliding scale. Sometimes we imagine that God views us as relatively good and sometimes as relatively bad. We think of our status with God as something like a dimmer switch, always fluctuating according to our performance.

Yet Paul says differently. He says our status with God is like an ordinary light switch. It's either on or off. In verse 21 we see the off position. Three descriptions: alienated, enemies and wicked. Nothing saintly about us!

What changes? Us? Do we embark on a little holiness project to turn things around? No. Here's what changes things. Christ works reconciliation between us and God. He comes as peacemaker. He takes our side, takes our flesh and puts our unholy humanity to death. Rising up by the power of the Holy Spirit, He is presented to the Father in a glorified humanity. When we, by that same Holy Spirit, are united to Jesus by faith, we too are presented to the Father *in Christ*. And now, how does God see us? Well Paul gives us another three descriptions, and how different they are: "holy, unblameable and unreproveable."

Not just blameless but unblameable. Not just without reproof, but unreproveable. God does not see us according to our unholiness. He sees us in Jesus and says to us – "you are holy."

Sainthood is not conferred by the church but by God. Sainthood is not earned by us, but worked on our behalf by Christ. And sainthood is not the preserve of monks and nuns. Sainthood is the status of the Christian – every Christian.

Forget dimmer-switch Christianity, if you belong to Jesus the light has been switched on. The decisive change *has* happened. You are not climbing a saintliness ladder. You are not walking a holiness tightrope. Whatever the world calls you, God calls you "holy, unblameable and unreproveable."

You're not just saintly. You might not *even* be saintly. But here's God's verdict, without a hint of irony or reserve, He says: "You're a saint!"

13 November – Romans 2:1-29

A law unto themselves

He's his own man. A 'loose canon', a 'live wire', 'off the radar'. Or in other words "a law unto himself." That's the way we tend to use the phrase nowadays.

Question: What would God prefer us to be? Would He rather we lived 'under the law' or would He rather we be 'a law unto ourselves'?

The surprising answer is that God wants us all to stop being under the law and instead to be a law unto ourselves! But we need to understand what the *Bible* means by these phrases.

Early in his letter to the Romans Paul declares the substance of his teaching:

> "I am not ashamed of the gospel of Christ: for it is the power of God unto salvation to every one that believeth; to the Jew first, and also to the Greek." (Romans 1:16)

Salvation comes from the Jews, so said Jesus said in John 4. They were the chosen people through whom the Messiah would come. But once He came, the nations (the Gentiles) would put their hope in Him. First the Jews, then the Gentiles. That's the way the gospel works.

But it is the *gospel* of Christ that saves the world and nothing else. That's why Paul immediately goes on to rule out any other way of salvation.

From chapter 1:18 all the way until chapter 3:20, Paul demolishes our confidence in *any* human identity or ability or performance. No nationality, no religion, no moral code, no deeds can avert the judgement that has rested upon our race since Adam. And every attempt to lift ourselves above condemnation through the law of God is like Baron Munchhausen trying to lift himself out of the swamp by his hair. It is futile and denies the seriousness of our predicament.

In Romans 2, Paul addresses the Jew who uses the law to feel superior to those without it. But their claim to special treatment is void. *Having* the law is one thing. Doing what it says is entirely another:

> "For as many as have sinned without law shall also perish without law: and as many as have sinned in the law shall be judged by the law; (For not the hearers of the law are just before God, but the doers of the law shall be justified. For when the Gentiles, which have not the law, do by nature the things contained in the law, these, having not the law, are **a law unto themselves**: Which shew the work of the law written in their hearts."
> (Romans 2:12-15)

So who are these Gentiles who are "a law unto themselves"? Well verse 15 uses the language of Jeremiah 31 to describe them: they are those with the law written on their hearts. In other words, these are the Gentiles who are cottoning onto salvation in Christ. They are coming into that global salvation which the Jewish Scriptures prophesied. The whole purpose of the law was to testify to Christ, and they were following the true intention of the law by trusting Him. Even though they never had the law of Moses (the old covenant), they are now enjoying the new covenant reality.

And the difference between the covenants is this: in the old covenant, God's life stood above, judging you for how far short you fell. In the new, the law is fulfilled and God's life is put within you. Law is not over you. You are a law unto yourself. You don't have a godly limit imposed on you, you have a godly impulse driving you.

According to Paul, if someone is "a law unto themselves" they are not unpredictable or unruly. Certainly they have escaped from being "under the law". But that has liberated them to be truly good. Not good so as to tick some boxes. Not good, so as to make some grade. But good from the heart.

God doesn't want anyone to be "under the law." He desires Jews and Gentiles – the whole world – to become a "law unto themselves." Christ didn't come to create "live wires" and rebels, that's not what the phrase means. To be a law unto yourself is to be liberated by Jesus from the external code and freed into the life of love which the law describes but can never produce. The gospel is the power of God to save us from petty legalisms and bring us into Christ's life, ruled from within not constrained from without. In short, the difference between 'under the law' and 'law unto yourself' is the difference between God on your back, and God on your side.

I know which I'd rather, and so does God!

14 November – Romans 3:21-4:25

Hope against hope

It's the hope you have when there is no hope.

Abraham was 99 years old and Sarah 90 when they were promised a miracle child (Isaac). As Genesis 18:11 put it: "Abraham and Sarah were old and well stricken in age; and it ceased to be with Sarah after the manner of women." Nonetheless, the promise came from the LORD. "Sarah thy wife shall have a son."

That's not just difficult, it's impossible. So what do you do when faced with the LORD's word on one hand and human impossibility on the other? You hope against hope:

> "Abraham, **against hope believed in hope**, that he might become the father of many nations, according to that which was spoken, So shall thy seed be. And being not weak in faith, he considered not his own body now dead, when he was about an hundred years old, neither yet the deadness of Sara's womb: He staggered not at the promise of God through unbelief; but was strong in faith, giving glory to God; And being fully persuaded that, what he had promised, he was able also to perform. And therefore it was imputed to him for righteousness."
> (Romans 4:18-22)

What does saving faith look like? Abraham's "hope against hope" is Paul's example. He is in the middle of a magisterial study of the gospel, showing how salvation comes not through our goodness but God's grace, not through our faithfulness but Christ's, not through our power but the Spirit's. Salvation is God's thing. It's not our thing. We simply receive a salvation that we could never earn.

And so Paul chooses an example of faith which is a true case of 'hope against hope.' Abraham is completely 'out of the driver's seat' when the

Lord comes to him. He not only *does* not meet the Lord half way, he cannot. All he can do is rest in the Lord's promise and say, "Amen, let it be so."

This is faith: the promise of new life comes and faith says "*Nothing* in my circumstances and nothing in my power can make this happen but, Lord, I know You can!" The promised seed is held out and faith says "*I* cannot produce the Messiah, indeed I am incapable of even *receiving* the Messiah, yet Lord, you say He is given to me, so I will trust You."

The context for faith is a dark and barren space. There is no possibility for life and yet exactly here the Lord promises it. Whether it's Sarah's barren womb, Mary's virgin womb, or Christ's virgin tomb – we're confronted with the deepest human weakness and the greatest divine strength. Faith here is a 'hope against hope', because faith is the opposite of sight (2 Corinthians 5:7). The circumstances look hopeless, yet faith is trusting the Lord's word and not our capacities. And actually, when we despair of our earthly hopes, that's when a true hope can arise.

If our hope was only as good as our own resources, we would be on shaky ground indeed. Imagine a faith in *human* power to triumph over the dark and barren space of the tomb! No, we trust God's power to do the impossible. That is far more solid ground. We thank God that He makes our hope more certain than any *earthly* possibilities. He wants our faith to rest on *His* power not ours.

It's a hope against hope that truly brings hope. At that point we rest our faith not in ourselves but in Christ, the God of Resurrection and the Lord of the Impossible.

No-one sums up this up better than John Calvin:

> "Everything by which we are surrounded conflicts with the promise of God. He promises us immortality, but we are encompassed with mortality and corruption. He pronounces that we are righteous in His sight, but we are engulfed in sin. He declares His favour and goodwill towards us, but we are threatened by the tokens of his wrath. What can we do? It is His will that we should shut our eyes to what we are and have, in order that nothing may impede or even check our faith in Him."

God forbid

It's a far from literal translation, but it traces all the way back to Tyndale and even to Wycliffe before him. "May it never be" would be a stricter rendering of the Greek, but "God forbid" has endured as a statement of indignant resolve. It occurs 26 times in the Bible, the majority of the uses are from Paul.

It was a common rhetorical device of Paul's to voice a possible objection to his teaching and then to reject it firmly:

> "Is the law sin? **God forbid.**" (Romans 7:7)
>
> "Is there unrighteousness with God? **God forbid.**" (Romans 9:14)
>
> "Hath God cast away his people? **God forbid.**" (Romans 11:1)
>
> "Is therefore Christ the minister of sin? **God forbid.**" (Galatians 2:17)

In today's phrase, both the question and the emphatic answer are vital to understand:

> "What shall we say then? Shall we continue in sin, that grace may abound? **God forbid.**" (Romans 6:1-2)

Paul expects an objection to his teaching. It's an objection for which every gospel preacher must be prepared. If a preacher is not faced by this objection, we may question whether they are really preaching the *gospel.*

The objection is this: "Shall we continue in sin, that grace may abound?"

If we preach Paul's gospel, people will ask us this question. Because it might sound to them as though God's free gift of salvation is magnified if we commit more and more sins. If Jesus 'picks up the tab' for our bad behaviour and if His payment on the cross is His glory, then we can make Christ look more glorious can't we? We can rack up an even bigger debt for Him to cover. Thus we might continue in sin so that His grace may abound.

Paul's answer to this is emphatic: God forbid! He rules such thinking out of court. But notice *why* such thinking is rejected. He continues…

> "How shall we, that are dead to sin, live any longer therein? Know ye not, that so many of us as were baptized into Jesus Christ were baptized into his death? Therefore we are buried with him by baptism into death: that like as Christ was raised up

> from the dead by the glory of the Father, even so we also should walk in newness of life. For if we have been planted together in the likeness of his death, we shall be also in the likeness of his resurrection: Knowing this, that our old man is crucified with him, that the body of sin might be destroyed, that henceforth we should not serve sin. For he that is dead is freed from sin." (Romans 6:2-7)

So often we think of salvation individualistically and impersonally. We think that God gives each of us a "thing" called "grace" or "salvation" or "forgiveness." It's like a blank cheque handed from heaven, underwritten by the infinite worth of Christ's blood. And so we run off to spend God's grace on our sinful pleasures. But no, God gives us a Person called Christ – a Person with whom we have been united. We have been baptised *into* Him, planted together with Him, crucified with Him, buried with Him and raised again to newness of life. We are not individuals with a "get out of hell card", we are members of Christ Himself, in Whom our sin and its consequences have been dealt with once and for all. We have been brought through sin and death out into new life.

We have not been saved *to* sin, we have been saved *from* sin – freed to live a new life. And not as individuals. We are in Christ, united to Him like a bride to a Bridegroom. And our heavenly Husband loves us to death. In that context sin is unthinkable!

Imagine two couples. Both of them have husbands who travel for business. Wife A says to her husband, "I know what happens on business trips. Your clients will take you to the restaurant and then the bar and who knows where from there. I've heard about these things, and you need to know that if you even look at another woman, this marriage is finished. Don't bother coming back. I'll change the locks, it's over mister!"

Wife B says "I know what happens on business trips. And if you stray I would be truly devastated. But when I said 'Till death us do part' I meant it. And whatever happens I want you to come home and be honest and I want you to know I love you always and we'll work it out."

Question: Which husband is more likely to cheat? Husband A every time.

We imagine that the way to make people good is to add conditions to the love of God. "God loves you a lot. But if you sin, the love cools and you'll have to mope around on the outskirts of His presence." Actually conditional love does not "keep us honest." Conditional love turns our hearts away from the Lover and towards other things. It's *un*conditional love that captures the heart. Christ grips us with a love that says "No matter where you go or what you do, I am with you and I am for you. We have an unbreakable marriage-bond and I love you come what may."

More than this, Christ has taken us through sin and its consequences and out into freedom. However we might muck around in the pit, Christ has lifted us to the throne. And whatever promises which sin makes – they are lies. The desires we seek to satisfy are truly met in our Loving Bridegroom. And He will never leave us or forsake us.

Therefore, shall we continue in sin, that grace may abound? **God forbid!**

16 November – Romans 6:1-23

The wages of sin is death

Driving across my wife's home town of Belfast, it's difficult not to come across this verse emblazoned on some billboard or other:

> "For the wages of sin is death; but the gift of God is eternal life through Jesus Christ our Lord." (Romans 6:23)

And it's usually in the King James Version too!

It serves as a succinct summary of the gospel as it outlines three contrasting pairs. There is wages versus gift, sin versus God and death versus eternal life.

On one side of the divide we have sin as a slave-master. This is how Paul has been portraying sin throughout Romans 6. It is not so much an action that we choose but a power that masters us. We're not in charge of sin, sin is in charge of us. But it's a law-abiding slave-master – it pays a wage. The whole realm in which sin operates is the realm of working and earning. This pay-master always gives his workers what's coming to them. And what is the payment? Death.

There's something very organic here. Sin is anti-life. It is shutting down from the life-giving Lord and trying to work things out from our own resources. When we serve this master we get what's coming to us – death.

But there's another way. Is it to just choose not to sin? Impossible. We are like Israel in Egypt – in slavery to a dark power that we can't overthrow. We need another Master to redeem us. But thankfully the second half of the verse gives us one: God! He is a very different Master. You see, in contrast to how we naturally think, *sin* is the kill-joy, God is the life-giver. Sin is the legalist, God is the gracious One. Sin demands that I *work* for a *wage*. God offers a *gift* by His *grace* – the Lord Jesus Christ. Sin is death-dealing. God is life-giving.

And again the outcome of serving *this* Master is organically related to who this master is. Since God *is* a Life-giving Fountain, pouring forth Himself in His Son and Spirit, therefore receiving *His* gift means receiving eternal life. It's just natural that *His* realm means receiving. And receiving God's kind of life is receiving eternal life.

Next time you are tempted to sin, remember it's bigger than you. Remember it's a master you have no power to overthrow. It's not your servant, it's a slave-master. It's not *offering* anything, it's taking. It's not bringing you into a realm of grace but only into the realm of works. And no matter what it promises, it's not giving you life but only death. On the other hand, God is offering you redemption, freedom, grace and eternal life through Jesus Christ our Lord.

Today spend a moment to re-orient your thinking according to the gospel. Take a moment to see yourself, to see sin and to see God again in light of Jesus Christ.

17 November – Romans 7:1-25

O wretched man that I am!

It was Jesus who coined the phrase "the Spirit is willing, the flesh is weak." It was Paul who explored the idea in chapter after chapter.

According to the Apostle Paul there are three tenses of salvation. There is the past tense:

> "According to God's mercy He saved us." (Titus 3:5)

There is the present tense:

> "The preaching of the cross is… unto us which ***are [being] saved***… the power of God." (1 Corinthians 1:18)

And there is the future tense:

> "We shall be saved from wrath through Jesus." (Romans 5:9)

How do we make sense of this? Well Paul also talks about three aspects to our humanity. There is our spirit, which is made righteous the moment we trust Christ:

> "The Spirit itself beareth witness with our spirit, that we are the children of God." (Romans 8:16)

There is our soul or mind (the Greek word is psyche). This is in the process of being transformed:

> "Be ye transformed by the renewing of your mind." (Romans 12:2)

And there is our flesh which remains unredeemed until Christ returns. Below is Paul's cry of anguish in Romans 7. Notice how his mind is on God's side. He *wants* to live righteously. He *agrees* that the law is good. But his flesh is the problem:

> "For we know that the law is spiritual: but I am carnal [i.e. fleshly], sold under sin. For that which I do I allow not: for what I would, that do I not; but what I hate, that do I. If then I do that which I would not, I consent unto the law that it is good. Now then it is no more I that do it, but sin that dwelleth in me. For I know that in me (that is, in my flesh,) dwelleth no good thing: for to will is present with me; but how to perform that which is good I find not. For the good that I would I do not: but the evil which I would not, that I do. Now if I do that I would not, it is no more I that do it, but sin that dwelleth in me. I find then a law, that, when I would do good, evil is present with me. For I delight in the law of God after the inward man: But I see another law in my members, warring against the law of my mind, and bringing me into captivity to the law of sin which is in my members. **O wretched man that I am! who shall deliver me from the body of this death?** I thank God through Jesus Christ our Lord. So then with the mind I myself serve the law of God; but with the flesh the law of sin." (Romans 7:14-25)

Do you hear the terrible struggle of the flesh and the Spirit? This is the Christian life according to Paul (he repeats the teaching in Galatians 5). We want to do good, we continue to do evil. We hate our sin, yet we can't seem to shake it. It clings to us, like skin to our bones.

What will deliver us?

The law? No, we might agree that it's right, but it has no power to effect what it commands. Some Christians teach that God gives us the Spirit so that we will have strength enough to perform the works of the law – and by *this* we are saved. Nonsense. The person with the Spirit may agree with the law, they may love the law, but the law itself plays no part in our salvation. It still only condemns us while-ever we remain in the flesh.

Can our will power deliver us? No, in our better moments our resolve is for righteousness, but we continue to be embroiled in wretched behaviour.

What will deliver us? Only "Jesus Christ our Lord" can deliver us. And notice, deliver us "from the *body* of this death." That's what the Christian awaits – the future tense salvation when not only our spirits and souls, but even our flesh is redeemed.

As chapter 8 will reveal, only resurrection will save us in that final, future sense. Jesus Himself has already risen beyond sin, wrath, death and law. But only when He returns to apply that resurrection reality to our *bodies* will we enter into the fullness of His salvation. Until then the normal Christian life is groaning, it's struggle. But it's also hope.

You see out of this wrestling, Paul pens one of the greatest verses of Christian assurance. *Because* he groans and struggles, he knows that the Spirit *is* in him, striving against the flesh. Thus, as counter-intuitive as it may seem, the conflict gives him confidence. And so he writes:

> "There is ***therefore*** now no condemnation to them which are in Christ Jesus." (Romans 8:1)

If you're stuck in the Christian life – hating your sin but seemingly powerless to change – look up. Christ alone is your hope. Nothing within you will save. But *He* will deliver you from this body of death. The day will come when we are righteous – body, soul and spirit – Hallelujah!

In the meantime, let the law speak to your flesh. Allow it's condemnation to fall upon that nature you inherited from Adam. It's going to perish anyway. Agree with the law and hate your sin. But never let the law and its condemnation speak to your conscience, your psyche, your mind. No, Adam no longer defines you. He may live on in your deeds, but you are no longer determined by him. Your true self is hidden in Christ. He is bigger than Adam. His salvation is stronger than your sin. His Spirit is greater than your flesh. And the conflict you feel is actually proof that you *have* the new life.

Therefore, sinning, struggling, groaning Christian – wretch that you are – there is now no condemnation for those who are in Christ Jesus.

Vengeance is mine

Belief in a God of vengeance will create vengeful people, right?

On the other hand, if we want to pursue peace ourselves, we must dispense with the view of God as some Settler of scores, right?

Actually the Apostle Paul argues precisely the opposite. He begins by enjoining an incredible level of pacifism on the Christian:

> "Recompense to no man evil for evil. Provide things honest in the sight of all men. If it be possible, as much as lieth in you, live peaceably with all men. Dearly beloved, avenge not yourselves." (Romans 12:17-19)

There's a realism here ("as much as lieth in you") but also a supernatural expectation: "live peaceably with all men." This is explicitly in the context of "evil" done to the Christian. This is the occasion when vengeance and wrath will be rising up in us. How on earth can we resist? Paul says, "Give place unto wrath:…

> " … for it is written, **Vengeance is mine; I will repay, saith the Lord**. Therefore if thine enemy hunger, feed him; if he thirst, give him drink: for in so doing thou shalt heap coals of fire on his head. Be not overcome of evil, but overcome evil with good." (Romans 12:17-21)

There is a "place" for wrath. But that place is not in our hands. We are no good at wrath. But God is. The whole practice of vengeance belongs to the Father Almighty. *He* takes care of the payback business. He's good at His job and He promises to settle scores with perfect justice. *Therefore*, says Paul, you are free to love your enemies in extraordinary and counter-conditional ways.

And it's God's *vengeance* that is the grounds for your peace-making. If that still sounds odd, perhaps we should allow Miroslav Volf to teach us. He is a Croatian theologian whose family and community saw terrible violence during the ethnic cleansing of the early 90s. He writes: "The practice of non-violence requires a belief in divine vengeance." He realises that we in the comfortable West may baulk at this. But he asks us to face the realities of evil which remain, for most of us, a distant theory.

> "Imagine speaking to people (as I have) whose cities and villages have been first plundered, then burned, and leveled to the ground, whose daughters and sisters have been raped, whose

> fathers and brothers have had their throats slit…Your point to them – we should not retaliate? Why not? I say – the only means of prohibiting violence by us is to insist that violence is only legitimate when it comes from God."

Only the God who is *good* at vengeance can enable a victim of evil to resist becoming a perpetrator. There is a judgement to come – a perfect righting of wrongs. There's no need for vigilantes. We can entrust all judgement to Christ who, through His cross, showed Himself perfect in justice.

But even more than this, when a Christian knows of the judgement to come, it can inspire something truly remarkable: pity for the evil-doer.

Corrie Ten Boom told the story of her imprisonment at Ravensbruck concentration camp in *The Hiding Place.* One day she and her sister, Betsie, were forced to watch a concentration camp matron beating a prisoner. "Oh, the poor woman," Corrie cried. "Yes. May God forgive her," Betsie replied.

Corrie was crying for the prisoner. Betsie was praying for the guard. That's the difference it makes to know that vengeance is the Lord's. For as their father had once said, "I pity the poor Germans, they have touched the apple of God's eye."

How can anyone pity a concentration camp guard? How can anyone pity the perpetrators of the holocaust? Only those who know there is a woe greater than Ravensbrook and a power far higher than the Nazis. In the light of *that* day, everyone becomes an object of our sympathy, even our foulest enemies. The vengeance of God makes peacemakers of us all.

19 November – Romans 13:1-14

The powers that be

Romans 13 has introduced two phrases to the world that seem to pull in different directions – at least in the way they are used.

On the one hand we have "the powers that be." We commonly use this phrase to describe nameless authorities handing down impersonal judgements:

> – "*Apparently, in their infinite wisdom, the powers that be have decided to scrap the old policy…*"

Faceless bureaucrats or untouchable rulers are "the powers that be." They are undefined in number, but definitely more than one (it's not "the power that is"!) We feel like they are answerable to no-one. They are *the powers*. And they seem, immovably, to *be* so. What is worse, Paul tells us to submit unquestioningly to them!

> "Let every soul be subject unto the higher powers. For there is no power but of God: **the powers that be** are ordained of God. Whosoever therefore resisteth the power, resisteth the ordinance of God: and they that resist shall receive to themselves damnation. For rulers are not a terror to good works, but to the evil. Wilt thou then not be afraid of the power? do that which is good, and thou shalt have praise of the same." (Romans 13:1-3)

Here is proof that Paul sometimes uses "damnation" and "wrath" in temporal ways. Governments might sentence you to prison, or even to execution, but they cannot sentence you to hell. Nonetheless there is a temporal respect to be paid to temporal rulers who hold temporal powers of punishment over us. And such an arrangement is not outside of God's sovereignty – "the powers that be are ordained of God!"

Oh dear – we might think – is Paul giving *carte blanche* to despots everywhere? Is he putting the seal of God's authority onto every tyranny that asserts itself?

Well consider the other influence Romans 13 has had on our language. Paul continues…

> "For he is the **minister** of God to thee for good. But if thou do that which is evil, be afraid; for he beareth not the sword in vain: for he is the **minister** of God, a revenger to execute wrath upon him that doeth evil. Wherefore ye must needs be subject, not only for wrath, but also for conscience sake. For for this cause pay ye tribute also: for they are God's **ministers**, attending continually upon this very thing. Render therefore to all their dues: tribute to whom tribute is due; custom to whom custom; fear to whom fear; honour to whom honour." (Romans 13:4-7)

The true status of a ruler is "minister", i.e. "servant". In the West we are used to considering our politicians as "ministers" and our chief ruler as *Prime* Minister. But such thinking should not be taken for granted – it is a deeply *Christian* conviction. There's nothing obvious about considering a ruler to be a servant and in non-Christian cultures the people have suffered for it.

And so Romans 13 actually provides a profound *challenge* to the powers that be. They are not ultimate powers at all. They are servants in the truest sense, and servants with a strictly limited scope – to execute temporal judgements on wrong-doers. There is an honour to be given them, but an honour in proportion to what is "due".

Thus the *citizen* reading Romans 13 is challenged to look beyond temporal rulers to God and His sovereign ordination. They are to render what is due to rulers, and not because they agree with them. In all likelihood the ruler on the throne as Paul wrote this was Nero! Yet even with such a despot, Paul calls them to live peaceably. As he writes in 1 Timothy 2:

> "I exhort therefore, that, first of all, supplications, prayers, intercessions, and giving of thanks, be made for all men; For kings, and for all that are in authority; that we may lead a quiet and peaceable life in all godliness and honesty. For this is good and acceptable in the sight of God our Saviour; Who will have all men to be saved, and to come unto the knowledge of the truth."
> (1 Timothy 2:1-4)

The truly revolutionary work, at which Christians should labour, is prayer and evangelism (notice how closely the peaceable life is linked to God's desire for salvation to spread). This is the work of the kingdom that outlasts all the powers that be. That should be our focus.

But for the *rulers* reading Romans 13 there is also great challenge. They are not to "lord it over" the people. They are to be servants. Because all rulers must take their cue from the King of kings:

> "Ye know that they which are accounted to rule over the Gentiles exercise lordship over them; and their great ones exercise authority upon them. But so shall it not be among you: but whosoever will be great among you, shall be your minister: And whosoever of you will be the chiefest, shall be servant of all. For even the Son of man came not to be ministered unto, but to minister, and to give his life a ransom for many."
> (Mark 10:42-45)

20 November – 1 Corinthians 1:1-2:5

Stumblingblock

What would convince the world to believe in God?

I once asked an atheist the question: "What would convince *you* to believe in God?" He answered:

"Until god appears before me as a burning bush or I see his picture on the front of popular science magazines I will remain a non-believer."

It strikes me that those two kinds of "evidence" represent the two kinds of ways the world looks for God. We either want the miracle-encounter or we want the rational proof. Both would be preferable, but usually people lean towards one kind of evidence or another.

Some of us say, "It doesn't have to make sense to me but if God just showed up in awesome wonder, if He just demonstrated His supernatural powers in some out-of-this-world miracle, that would do it for me." Others would say, "I don't need a burning bush, just show me the equations, take me through the logical arguments, give me the scientific proof, demonstrate that it's *reasonable*, then I'll believe."

As Paul wrote to Christians in Corinth he recognised these two kinds of thinking. He identified the "power" people with the Jews and the "wisdom" people with the Greeks. This makes sense. The Jews were a people with whom God had been very hands-on. They were a people to whom God had shown up in mighty acts and so they were a people that came to expect miraculous signs. On the other hand the Greeks had been left to piece things together from a distance. They were used to trusting their own minds to reveal the truth. Therefore, says Paul:

> "The Jews require a sign, and the Greeks seek after wisdom." (1 Corinthians 1:22)

Notice that both the "power" people and the "wisdom" people are making demands of God. They are both saying to God, "These are the terms by which I am prepared to do business with you." Yet Paul says that God is in the business of frustrating all such demands. He goes on…

> "But we preach Christ crucified, unto the Jews a **stumblingblock**, and unto the Greeks foolishness." (1 Corinthians 1:23)

Here is the way God shows up: In a world full of power-lovers and wisdom-seekers, He shows up on a cross. It's not the way anyone expected. And it's not the way anyone wants. In fact it is scandalous to the world.

The word "stumblingblock" is a translation of the Greek work *skandalon.* It's something that causes you to trip up. But this is how God wants it. For a people looking up for signs in the sky, God wants a big rock laid in their path so that they stumble and fall. For a people looking down into their microscopes or fine tuning their logical arguments, He confronts them, not with something obviously *wiser*, but with something blatantly foolish.

The miracle-lover is given weakness – a bloodied corpse on a cross. The wisdom-seeker is given foolishness – a God who dies! It is precisely what they didn't want. Yet it's just what God wants preached.

Therefore those who preach Christ should be prepared to be scorned as the most frustrating, bemusing, scandalous, pathetic God-peddlers imaginable. Christian preachers simply do not give people what they want. They are forever laying before the world a giant stumblingblock.

But in the next verse, there's a *true* miracle that can happen.

> "But unto them which are called, both Jews and Greeks, Christ the power of God, and the wisdom of God."
> (1 Corinthians 1:24)

Here is the greatest miracle imaginable: someone can stumble upon the cross and say: "My Lord and My God!" In amidst this perishing world, someone can see the perishing LORD and say, "*There* is God's power and wisdom."

Because it *is* powerful. Immensely powerful. Any old despot can rule *over* people. What kind of strength does it take to serve *beneath* them? Any old debater can out-argue another. What kind of wisdom does it take to subvert every term of the discussion and turn the arguments right-side-up? That's what the cross does. It shows a greater power and a deeper wisdom, not by agreeing with the world's definitions but by revolutionising them. As verse 25 says:

> "Because the foolishness of God is wiser than men; and the weakness of God is stronger than men."

There is an incomparable wisdom and strength to the cross – death defeated through dying, the curse conquered through condemnation, the devil vanquished by losing, the Son glorified in shame. It's the wisdom that is not built upon human foundations, rather it undermines every human foundation. It's the strength that overpowers by surrender, disarming every show of earthly force. When a person stumbles over the cross and sees it for its *true* wisdom and power, they are won by a very different God.

You see the living God can never be found by the earthly search for power and wisdom. Because the *living* God is not a super-human. He's not like us just with a few more muscles or brain-cells. But our sinful selves would love it if He were. We have a lot invested in thinking of God as some super-despot. In many ways, that would suit us just fine because then we'd be justified in seeking to be rid of Him.

One atheist told me he'd believe in God if He made the stars to spell out the ten commandments in the sky. But what a dreadful god that would be! Such a god simply stays at a distance, pulls off some magic tricks (that are no good to anyone), and is basically interested in making us behave. If God were like that we'd have every reason to hate and run from Him.

But this is why it's imperative to lay the stumblingblock in people's way. If natural man is seeking a god, it can only be an idol. We must give them Christ crucified. There on the cross is the living God – the God who does not stay at a distance, the God who does not glorify Himself with cheap magic tricks, the God who is not basically concerned with keeping us moral. No, this God draws near. This God stoops and serves and bleeds and dies. And He does it not to enforce our goodness but to forgive our badness.

Never give people what they want. Give them Christ crucified. When they stumble over the cross they'll see a God more wonderful than anything they'd imagined.

21 November – 1 Corinthians 7:1-40

The time is short

> "I have discovered that all the unhappiness of men arises from one single fact, that they cannot stay quietly in their own chamber."

So said French mathematician and Christian thinker Blaise Pascal. Therefore, said Pascal, we fill our lives with diversions so that we might distract ourselves from "our feeble and mortal condition."

In other words, we humans are a restless bunch. The married want to be single, the single want to be married. One worker wants to be free of work, the unemployed man just wants a job. We are forever looking ahead and thinking "if only", or backwards and thinking "those were the days." We find it almost impossible to settle in the here and now.

The Corinthians were no different. In 1 Corinthians 7 Paul addresses a restless church and his overwhelming message is "Stay put!" And this was his message because these Christians were anything but content.

You see married people didn't want to act married (v1-5); those married to unbelievers didn't want to stick with their spouses (v10-16); single people didn't want to be single (v6-9, 25-40); slaves didn't want to remain in their duties (v20-24) and even the circumcised wanted to become uncircumcised (v17-19). How restless do you have to be to want to alter your circumstances at *that* level.

But Paul's message is emphatic: Stay put! It's not a hard and fast rule. There are many examples within the chapter of people changing their life circumstances (e.g. v21 or v36). But as a rule of thumb Paul says, Stay put where God has you.

He has three reasons for this:

First he says, "Remember your calling"

> "As the Lord hath called every one, so let him walk." (1 Corinthians 7:17)
>
> "Let every man abide in the same calling wherein he was called." (1 Corinthians 7:20)
>
> "Brethren, let every man, wherein he is called, therein abide with God." (1 Corinthians 7:24)

God has called you into fellowship with His Son, Jesus (1 Corinthians 1:9). And, Corinthians, He's done it while you have been in the midst of any and every circumstance. Therefore your life situation is not the point. Fellowship with Jesus is the point. And you can have that while married or single, slave or free, circumcised or uncircumcised. If you're not content in Christ then getting married/divorced or changing jobs won't solve it. There's nothing in your circumstances you need to change. Flee sin, but don't flee your situation.

The second reason we should as a rule, stay put, is evangelism. As we build up a witness in one station in life it can have a tremendous impact on those around us (e.g. v16).

Thirdly we should generally stay put because "the time is short."

> "But this I say, brethren, **the time is short**: it remaineth, that both they that have wives be as though they had none; And they that weep, as though they wept not; and they that rejoice, as though they rejoiced not; and they that buy, as though they possessed not; And they that use this world, as not abusing it: for the fashion of this world passeth away. But I would have you without carefulness." (1 Corinthians 7:29-32)

Paul is not advocating the abandonment of our marital and other duties (he does the very opposite in this chapter). But he is saying: Don't live for your marriage. Don't live for the idea of getting married. Don't live for your job. And don't live for your kids. Don't live for that relationship. Don't live for that achievement or that possession or that feeling. Live for that Day when everything you've lost will be more than made up for and when everyone you love will face Jesus. Live for that Day because the time is short.

When we hear that "the time is short" we usually think "Yikes, I'd better run around and get as many experiences as I can." But that's only because we think that our time *to live* is running out. Paul is saying the opposite. The way he thinks about it, time is short *and then* we will really live. Not long now and we'll inherit immortal bodies, explore a glorious new creation, be released from every burden and labour, and enjoy the ultimate marriage with Christ forever. Not long now until life really begins. The time in which you're asked to stick at that difficult job, that difficult marriage, that difficult singleness, it's only short. Relatively speaking!

Are you restless in your work, your home, your marriage, your singleness? Do you peer over the fence with longing, thinking you'll be happy if only you have *that* job, *that* relationship, *that* set of circumstances. Those things will never satisfy. We are not to set our hearts on them.

As we battle discontent, it may be that the Lord will bring us out of our current life circumstances. But that is not our hope. Instead, we seek to know Jesus in the place where we are. We seek to witness to Him in the here and now. And we take heart, the time is short: Soon and very soon, we are going to see the Lord!

22 November – 1 Corinthians 9:1-27

All things to all men

When we hear the phrase we think of two-faced gossips, slick marketing men or political spin doctors. Actually Paul is speaking about a ministry philosophy of deep integrity. He's talking about a flexibility that seeks to honour something far deeper than cultural expressions.

In 1 Corinthians 9 the Apostle is laying bare his *modus operandi.* He is discussing how it is that he can move so freely from one culture to the next – from stern religionists in the synagogue, to free-thinking philosophers at the Areopagus, to the common people in the market-place. In every situation he adopts cultural practices that are appropriate. Why? Is he a people-pleasing chameleon? Does he not know who he is? Actually it's because he *does* know his true identity that Paul is so able to adapt. *Because* he belongs to Christ he is free from the claims of culture. Yet, being free, he uses it to serve:

> "Though I be free from all men, yet have I made myself servant unto all, that I might gain the more. And unto the Jews I became as a Jew, that I might gain the Jews; to them that are under the law, as under the law, that I might gain them that are under the law; To them that are without law, as without law, (being not without law to God, but under the law to Christ,) that I might gain them that are without law. To the weak became I as weak, that I might gain the weak: I am made **all things to all men**, that I might by all means save some." (1 Corinthians 9:19-22)

Let me ask you a question: What does a Christian look like?

The scandal is – everyone knows what a Christian looks like: Ned Flanders. Christians look white, middle-class, suburban, university educated, sanctimonius and deeply irritating. Of course statistically that's nonsense. Within my own denomination – Anglicanism – the average worshipper is a 20-something Nigerian woman who has to travel more than 2 miles to get clean water. But nonetheless, the stereotype persists. And it's a scandal because the gospel stands above culture.

You actually can't answer the question "What does a Christian look like?" You might ask "What does a Christian *act* like?" But you'd get the answer "Jesus." More specifically, "The Jesus who hung out with prostitutes, publicans and sinners, even as he mingles with Pharisees and preaches in the synagogue." You see *Jesus* was all things to all men that some might be saved. His people follow suit.

That doesn't mean we are all spin and no substance. Even when Paul enters deeply into another culture there is still something ruling Paul. In verse 21 he says he's not free from God's law but he uses a wonderful phrase to describe his relationship to Christ. The Greek could literally be translated: "I am in-lawed by Christ." Not that Christ is like the in-laws – that would not be good! It's the idea of Paul sunk down into Christ. Christ is Paul's law. Christ Himself is the ruling authority in Paul's life – Christ has en-law-ed Paul.

So Paul has not just cast off every rule and authority. He is ruled, he has a centre, he has integrity. It's Jesus.

Which means Paul could never say 'I became a drug dealer in order to win drug dealers.' 'I became a drug user to win drug users.' Or 'I became sex worker to win sex workers.' But it will mean some people saying 'I hang out with drug dealers and drug users to win drug dealers and drug users.' 'I hang out with sex workers to win sex workers.'

But why? Why go through all of this? It's so much easier to stick with people like us.

We strongly we gravitate towards 'people like us'. When we've walked into a room we've assessed those present in a nanosecond. Without even thinking about it, we strike up a conversation with people our age, our race, our tax bracket, our sense of humour, our fashion sense. We've made those calculations at the speed of thought, and we slot instantly into cliques. Because we crave acceptance, we deeply want to belong and it's exhausting crossing social and cultural boundaries.

So how does Paul do it? Well first he knows that he is unshakably one of the "in" crowd. Paul uses the phase "in Christ" over 150 times in his letters. It is the ultimate "inner ring" to belong to. And Paul is constantly reminding himself and his readers that we are *in* with regards to the one club that really counts. If the Father Almighty accepts us *in* the Beloved (Ephesians 1:6) we are free from the need for acceptance with others.

But more than this, in verse 23 Paul lets us in on his motivation: "this I do for the gospel's sake, that I might be partaker thereof with you."

Paul does not want to enjoy the gospel on his own. His vision of the future is to sit at Christ's table *with* the religious and the irreligious, the moral and the immoral, the cultured Greeks and the Barbarians alike. With that goal in mind, Paul reaches out with a gospel that is big enough to meet and change *anyone.*

Who do you want to sit down with on that day? Jesus has crossed the ultimate barriers to offer salvation to the world. His blood has paid for every tribe, language, people and tongue. Today we can join Him in reaching out. Let us become all things to all men that by all means we might save some.

23 November – 1 Corinthians 12:1-13:3

A faith that can move mountains

Together with the 23rd Psalm, and perhaps John chapter 1, *First Corinthians 13* is among the most popular chapters in the Bible. It is read at weddings and at funerals, at state ceremonies, hospital bedsides, school assemblies. It is the go-to Scripture for any and every occasion. It is often simply known as St Paul's "love chapter". And people think of it as a kind of Scriptural bubble-bath – warm and soothing and inoffensive.

In fact, it's nothing of the sort! When the Corinthians read this portion of Paul's letter, they would have been devastated, angered, rebuked and only *then* comforted. For the Corinthians – and for us when we've read it properly – this chapter is nothing like a bubble-bath. It's more like a scalding hot bath full of antiseptic! It exposes our cuts and bruises. 1 Corinthians 13 *hurts*.

In its first paragraph (verses 1-3) it revolutionises our thinking. In its second paragraph (verses 4-7) it strips us bare. Only in the final paragraph (verses 8-13) are we given hope.

Today let's look at this first paragraph:

> "Though I speak with the tongues of men and of angels, and have not charity, I am become as sounding brass, or a tinkling cymbal. And though I have the gift of prophecy, and understand all mysteries, and all knowledge; and though **I have all faith, so that I could remove mountains**, and have not charity, I am nothing. And though I bestow all my goods to feed the poor, and though I give my body to be burned, and have not charity, it profiteth me nothing." (1 Corinthians 13:1-3)

The Corinthians thought of themselves as *very* spiritual. They loved supernatural signs, hidden wisdom, ecstatic encounters, incommunicable mysteries, uncontrollable experiences. But Paul will say in this chapter that such 'spirituality' is utterly bankrupt without love (or charity as the KJV perhaps unhelpfully has rendered it). He dreams up the most spiritually gifted people imaginable only to say that such people are *nothing* without love.

In verse 1 we meet **the ecstatic worshipper**. He speaks in indecipherable languages and everyone is very impressed. Except God. To God it's like a "sounding brass or a tinkling cymbal." All noise and no love. Here is an empty spirituality – self-focused, proud and loveless.

In verse 2 we have another spiritual caricature – **the profound prophet**. The kind of person who sweeps up into the pulpit and knows Greek and Hebrew and they can quote Augustine in Latin and give examples from Homer the poet *and* Homer the Simpson.

In addition, this person has incredible leadership skills. That's what it means to have 'a faith that can move mountains'. Here is a leader that can inspire and direct people towards a goal. The leader sees the potential, trusts that it's the way forward and they can motivate many to share in the vision. Their faith moves mountains.

We are mightily impressed by the profound prophet – a spiritual leader with intelligence and authority. But, again, God is not impressed. If such a person has not love they are nothing. They are a spiritual zero. They do not show up on Jesus' radar screen.

Paul's teaching here is dynamite. What he is saying is this: there are gifted leaders in Christian ministry who are not Christians. They are nothing. They have the *gifts* of the Spirit but not the Spirit Himself. Without love, gifts mean *nothing.*

Now do you start to see why this chapter is not a bubble-bath? It is profoundly disturbing. Paul is saying that people can exercise incredible gifts within the church yet not actually belong to Jesus. (Of course Jesus says the same thing in Matthew 7:21-23). How do we respond to this?

Well perhaps we think, 'I know what Paul is saying: We need to stop investing in the flashy super-natural gifts and get on with sacrificial service.' Is that it? No, he's not saying that either. Look at verse 3…

In verse 3 we see another caricature: **the stoic do-gooder**. Paul imagines this no-nonsense servant giving away everything – even their very life – *ostensibly* in the cause of the kingdom. And yet, it's possible to do all this without love. There is loveless sacrifice. (That's why 'charity' is a poor translation. Charitable works are not the point at all, it's *love* that counts).

Love is not simply a 'decision of the will.' Love is not reducible to acts of service. You can choose to do outwardly loving things and still not *have* love.

And what do you get for it? Nothing. Again, *this* kind of spiritual person does not show up on God's radar.

How do you picture a properly spiritual person? What is it to be a Christian who is *really* 'going for it'? Some of us will picture the ecstatic worshipper, some of us will picture the profound prophet, some of us will picture the stoic-do-gooder. Paul says we are all wrong. *All* of those people – even if they are incredibly gifted at what they are doing – have missed the point entirely. The point is love.

Do you see how *absolutely necessary* love is? Not groovy experiences, not profound thoughts, not busy service – actual *love.* Love for Jesus and love for others. Love is the source and substance of the Christian life. Without it we are not even Christians.

When someone asks you how you are going in the Christian life, how do you tend to answer? Some will speak of their experiences, some of their gifted ministry, some of their sacrificial service, but those are not true barometers of our spiritual life. Those things are not connected to the state of our soul. Such gifts and performances might be in over-drive and yet we have missed the main thing. Is the love of Jesus in you? And does it come out of you? Those are the questions we should be asking.

This chapter is not a bubble-bath. It's a deeply uncomfortable antiseptic bath and it exposes all sorts of wounds. But in future posts we will see healing too…

24 November – 1 Corinthians 13:1-13

Beareth all things, believeth all things, hopeth all things, endureth all things

First Corinthians 13 is dynamite. It explodes every myth humanity has ever bought about spirituality.

As we saw last time, Paul holds out three models of super-spirituality: the ecstatic worshipper, the profound prophet and the stoic do-gooder. And he then detonates a bomb under each of them. *None* of these super-saints are *anything* if they don't have love. *Love* is the source and substance of the Christian life.

Well then, what *is* this love of which Paul speaks? In the second paragraph (verses 4-8), we will see that the love we must have is *completely* beyond us!

> "Charity suffereth long, and is kind; charity envieth not; charity vaunteth not itself, is not puffed up, Doth not behave itself unseemly, seeketh not her own, is not easily provoked, thinketh no evil; Rejoiceth not in iniquity, but rejoiceth in the truth; Beareth all things, believeth all things, hopeth all things, endureth all things. Charity never faileth." (1 Corinthians 13:4-8)

In verse 4 we read that love "suffereth long *and* is kind." That's an amazing combination. Some of us can do grim-faced patience… but it's not kind. Some of us can do superficial sweetness… but it's short-lived. Can you do longsuffering *and* kindness? Together?

Patience is a key element to the love Paul speaks of. He begins this paragraph with it and also ends with it: "Charity never faileth."

Love puts up with constant frustration, constant interruption, constant set-back, constant opposition. But in the midst of all that: Love *never* fails.

I sometimes think I'm loving - until someone asks of me just one thing too many. Or I'm serving one person, and suddenly another need comes from elsewhere. At that point, I'm tempted to snap at them: "Go away! Don't you realise I'm being *loving* over here?!"

Then in verse 4 Paul begins speaking of what love is *not.* And of course everything that love is not, the Corinthians are. Paul knows that the Corinthians *are* envying, boastful, puffed up, etc, etc. And, if we're honest, so are we.

We manage both to envy *and* to vaunt (verse 4). It should be impossible to be both, but somehow we manage it! We have feelings of inferiority and superiority simultaneously. We are able to think *both*: "I'm better than everyone" *and* at the same time think "It's not fair, I wish I was like them!"

And this is the polar opposite of love. Love is so consumed with the other person it is simply not interested in inferiority or superiority. Love doesn't think more of yourself, or less of itself, it just thinks of itself less! When love is flourishing, vaunting and envy are non-issues. But vaunting and envy are huge issues for us, so what does that say about us?

Verse 5 speaks of *not* being easily provoked. How do we fare at that one?

We all think we're easy-going until we're wronged. Then we see just how self-seeking we are. We snap, we're rude, we get angry and we keep score. That's what we're like. What would it be like to never be rude, never self-seeking, not easily angered, to never keep a record of wrong or bear a grudge. That's what love is.

How do you compare to verse 6? Do you ever wish evil on your opponents? Do you ever wish you could bend or hide or side line the truth because it's inconvenient? Love never does that.

And what about verse 7 – our famous saying for today? It's a lovely sentiment isn't it. Love "beareth all things, believeth all things, hopeth all things, endureth all things." Wonderful! But do you? Do you bear, believe, hope and endure through all times and in all circumstances? Be honest!

Love does.

I don't.

But this puts us onto something vital in this chapter. Consider the way Paul is describing love.

Superficially, it may look like 'charity' is an abstract noun with a lot of adjectives attached. But look again.

"Charity" here is a concrete, living thing that *performs* certain actions. Love is a power with a life of its own. Love is a Person.

But He's not you. And He's not me. So who is He?

The night before Jesus died, He entered a garden called Gethsemane and agonized in prayer. His soul was overwhelmed with sorrow to the point of death. He was sweating blood as He faced the prospect of the cross. It was, for Jesus, a cup of suffering too terrible to contemplate. And yet if He did not drink down the furious anger of God, we would have to. The dilemma was this – either Jesus goes to hell or we do. And in that garden Jesus said 'Let it be me.'

You see, "*Jesus* suffereth long, He is kind; He envieth not; He vaunteth not Himself. He is not puffed up. *Christ* doth not behave Himself unseemly, He seeketh not His own, is not easily provoked, and thinketh no evil. Our Lord rejoiceth not in iniquity, but rejoiceth in the truth; *He* beareth all things, believeth all things, hopeth all things, endureth all things. *Jesus* never faileth."

We often think of the question 'What is love?' Perhaps a better question is: Who is love?

Love is a Person. A Person who first has loved you.

1 John 4:19 sums up an absolutely fundamental bible truth: "We love God because He first loved us." Love is a Person, who has acted for you. He has done verses 4-7 for you. Therefore we are on the receiving end of this love.

Love is first something done *to* you. And then love is something done *in* … and *through* you.

That's why verses 1-3 talk about having love or not having love. It's one or the other. Do you have love or don't you? That's the big question for Paul. He does not ask: How loving are you on a scale of 1-10? Paul's interest – the Holy Spirit's interest – is in one thing: Do you have Love? There is a Person called Love, His name is Jesus and He has loved you incredibly.

Do you have Love?

25 November – 1 Corinthians 13:1-13

Now we see through a glass darkly

How would you compare life *now* to life when Jesus returns?

So often we think of 'the here and now' as the concrete reality and Christ's future as an ephemeral, 'wafty' hope. Paul thought of things precisely the other way around.

In the final paragraph of First Corinthians 13, Paul addresses our future hope. When compared to life in the presence of Jesus, it's our present experiences that are insubstantial:

> "Charity never faileth: but whether there be prophecies, they shall fail; whether there be tongues, they shall cease; whether there be knowledge, it shall vanish away. For we know in part, and we prophesy in part. But when that which is perfect is come, then that which is in part shall be done away. When I was a child, I spake as a child, I understood as a child, I thought as a child: but when I became a man, I put away childish things. For now we see through a glass, darkly; but then face to face: now I know in part; but then shall I know even as also I am known."
> (1 Corinthians 13:8-12)

Paul uses three illustrations to compare 'now' and 'then'.

In verse 10 he calls the future: '**perfection**.' It's the idea of everything brought to the goal for which it was designed. Right now all things are subjected to frustration. But then, our bodies will work the way they were meant to work. Relationships will work the way they are meant to work. The world will work the way it's meant to work. Perfection. You *are* built for it. It *is* coming.

Verse 11 describes our future as '**maturity**.' Paul says, we are like children now. Even the wisest and most knowledgeable among us are like babbling toddlers compared to our wisdom and maturity then.

In chapter 15 Paul will tell us that we are like seeds that die, go into the ground and rise up again. When we rise we will be immeasurably more glorious than how we have gone down. Now we are acorns. Then we will be oaks. We will grow up in every dimension. Maturity beyond our wildest dreams.

And then verse 12 we see the heart of our future: '**Face to face**'.

We've thought before about 'face to face' with Jesus. It's about closeness, transparency, openness, adoration, intimacy. Right now "we see through a glass darkly". We see Christ, but it's frustratingly indistinct. We have foretastes of paradise but they are a poor reflection.

We readily think that *now* we experience life in technicolor. We can only imagine an after-life in shades of grey. Paul says no. Right now it's like wearing a greased-up pair of sunglasses. Everything *now* is indistinct and shadowy. When Christ returns we will do life in High Definition. And what we will see is not just beauty – we will see Jesus. That is the heart of our future hope.

Every kiss you have ever desired, every affirmation you have ever craved, every relationship you have ever wanted, every success you have ever pursued, every longing you have ever felt is like seeing 'through a glass darkly.' Yet one day such desires will be met and surpassed. Life will *begin* when you are face to face with Jesus.

26 November – 1 Corinthians 13:1-14:5

Faith, hope and love ...

Heaven is a world of love. So said Jonathan Edwards in a famous sermon by that title. His text was our verse for today:

> "And now abideth faith, hope, charity, these three; but the greatest of these is charity." (1 Corinthians 13:13)

It's a trio that Paul uses often in his letters to describe the Christian life. Here he names the greatest of them. "Love" is what will characterise the world to come more than anything else. And so verse 13 brings this chapter full circle. Paul began by berating the Corinthians for their neglect of love. As we saw, they held up the ecstatic worshipper, the profound prophet and the stoic do-gooder, as their models of true spirituality. But Paul maintains that none of these mean anything without love.

He concludes by looking to the future and judging our present priorities in *that* light. If heaven is a world of love, how can we claim to be heavenly and yet loveless? And when we know that a heaven of love is coming, how can we spend our time investing in gifts and outwards performances?

As he says from verse 8:

> "Charity never faileth: but whether there be prophecies, they shall fail; whether there be tongues, they shall cease; whether there be knowledge, it shall vanish away. For we know in part, and we prophesy in part. But when that which is perfect is come, then that which is in part shall be done away." (1 Corinthians 13:8-10)

Gifts are like a torchlight. A torchlight in the dark is useful. But at noon, blazing sunshine swallows up the torchlight. In the same way, we are heading towards something so glorious that it swallows up our paltry gifts. Even the most dazzling and impressive gift today will be utterly obsolete when Christ's future comes to pass.

Can any of us imagine being face to face with Jesus and saying: *Hey Jesus, watch me speak in tongues! Hey Jesus, let me tell you my wisdom! Hey Jesus, listen to me preach!* No. We will shut our mouths. And we will gaze – face to face.

The life to come is a world of love. Allow Jonathan Edwards' description to whet your appetite:

> "Love is always a sweet principle; and especially divine love. This, even on earth, is a spring of sweetness; but in heaven it shall become a stream, a river, an ocean! All shall stand about the God of glory, who is the great fountain of love, opening, as it were, their very souls to be filled with those effusions of love that are poured forth from His fullness, just as the flowers on the earth, in the bright and joyous days of spring, open their bosoms to the sun, to be filled with His light and warmth, and to flourish in beauty and fragrancy under His cheering rays.
>
> "…And thus they will love, and reign in love… and thus in the full sunlight of the throne, enraptured with joys that are forever increasing, and yet forever full, they shall live and reign with God and Christ forever and ever!" From "Heaven, A World of Love"

We have seen the future. And the future is love. Therefore let us not be dazzled by the torchlights of our paltry gifts and performances. Instead let us live in the sunshine. And let us pass it on.

At the end of the day *only* love counts.

27 November – 1 Corinthians 15:1-58

O death where is thy sting?

When Monty Python's Life of Brian came out 30 years ago it caused a tremendous stir.

Now there are definitely reasons to object to the film. But we should not object simply because the film makes fun of religious people. *Jesus* made fun of religious people. Constantly. (e.g. The Mote and the Beam or Straining at a gnat).

No the problem with the *Life of Brian* is not that it *is* a comedy. Its biggest problem is that it's *not* a comedy. It is, finally, a complete tragedy. Its hero – Brian – is crucified and there is no rescue, no resurrection. Just a catchy song whistled from the cross…

Always look on the bright side of death,
just before you draw your terminal breath…

Life is quite absurd
And death's the final word…

You'll see it's all a show,
keep 'em laughing as you go,
just remember that the last laugh is on you…

There's the old saying: "Whoever laughs last, laughs loudest." Well here's the gospel according to *Monty Python* – death has the last laugh. And if that's true, all comedy is *black* comedy. All humour is *gallows* humour. It's about whistling through the graveyard to keep up your spirits. But life itself is not a comedy. Life is a tragedy and, if we can, we grab a few moments of joy while we await the inevitable.

Yet Paul in 1 Corinthians 15 has good news for us. Brian may have perished, but Christ rose again from the dead. And in the twinkling of an eye He will return to apply that resurrection power to the whole universe.

Which means that death does not have the last laugh. No, the Christian – even as they await their own certain death – can laugh at the grave.

> "O death, where is thy sting? O grave, where is thy victory?" (1 Corinthians 15:55)

This is incredible cheek. Death has conquered every human who has ever lived. The grave swallows us all. We don't have a hope in the world, and yet, here is the most audacious taunt. It's like David against Goliath, gloating about a victory that seems impossible. How can Paul speak like this?

Well he continues:

> "The sting of death is sin; and the strength of sin is the law. But thanks be to God, which giveth us the victory through our Lord Jesus Christ." (1 Corinthians 15:56-57)

The victory doesn't belong to us, it belongs to Jesus. He has submitted to death, pushed on through the grave and out the other side into immortal life. He has drawn the sting of death and risen again as the Firstfruits of a bumper crop of resurrection. When we are united to Jesus we share in both His death *and* His risen life.

Yes we will enter death. But the sting is drawn by Christ. For us it will not be the curse of godforsakenness. For us it will be 'falling asleep in Jesus.' And death will not have the last word. It does not have the victory – Christ does.

We must ask ourselves – what story do we inhabit? Is this a tragedy where death laughs at us? Or do we live in a cosmic comedy where we laugh at death?

Incredibly it's the latter. We don't cower before death. We don't make a few nervous jokes in the face of the inevitable. We can look death square in the eye and laugh at it. Life is a glorious and eternal comedy. And all's well that ends well.

> "Thanks be to God, which giveth us the victory through our Lord Jesus Christ." (1 Corinthians 15:57)

28 November – 2 Corinthians 3:1-18

The letter of the law

> – The fat-cat who exploits every tax loop-hole imaginable…
>
> – The hospital which lets pedantic box-ticking get in the way of patient-care…
>
> – The cricketer whose legal ploy is nonetheless "not cricket" (New Zealanders will never forgive Australians for this one!)…

In all these cases we'd say they obeyed the letter of the law but not the spirit.

2 Corinthians 3 seems to be the origin of the phrase. But perhaps even earlier, Christ's dealings with the Pharisees speak to this theme…

> "Woe unto you, scribes and Pharisees, hypocrites! for ye pay tithe of mint and anise and cummin, and have omitted the weightier matters of the law, judgment, mercy, and faith: these ought ye to have done, and not to leave the other undone." (Matthew 23:23)

These people are fastidious about certain aspects of the law – the parts that are most easily and visibly fulfilled. But they have no concern for "the weightier matters." The law is concerned with justice, mercy and faith, yet these are too costly and hidden for the Pharisees. Jesus doesn't use the phrase but we might say that they obey the letter but not the spirit of the law. Yet it's in 2 Corinthians 3 that Paul speaks particularly of the letter of the law.

> "[We are] ministers of the new testament; not of the letter, but of the spirit: for the letter killeth, but the spirit giveth life." (2 Corinthians 3:6)

The letter sets out the expectations of the law. And we're not meant to bemoan its requirements as petty. The law is glorious (v9-10). Yet its effect on us law-breakers is death.

Sometimes I will listen to a sermon that "lays down the law" and then overhear congregation members saying to the preacher "You really stepped on our toes this morning."

The kind of Christian life preached here is one in which the law *inconveniences*. It may even *wound* or *weigh down*. Yet, fundamentally, I am left alive and kicking. And after my wounding I am resolved to grit my teeth and try harder. Thus I leave church feeling 'challenged', 'rebuked' and 'determined to lift my game.'

Yet, according to the Bible, the purpose of the 'letter' is not to step on our toes. It is to kill! The old covenant was a "ministration of death" (v7). We don't simply feel inconvenienced by the letter of the law. We are slain by the glorious law of life which uncovers and judges us. There is no realm of self-respect left by which we pull ourselves together and get back in the game. No, we are obliterated by the law – that is its purpose.

Therefore what is our hope? Well our hope can't come from ourselves. And it can't come from the law either. It's interesting that Paul does not contrast the letter with the spirit of the *law*. Instead he contrasts it with the Spirit of the LORD (v16, 17). That's a vital difference.

Paul does not preach against literalistic fulfilment of the law only to endorse another kind of legalism! He doesn't say "don't get hung up on details, just obey the vibe." No, we look away from the law to another Source of life. The Spirit we are to receive is the Spirit of Christ – He is the One who fulfils the law. And He brings life where the letter brought only death.

If you want deep and abiding change in the Christian life, don't gaze at yourself. Don't gaze at the law. Don't even gaze at the spirit of the law. Gaze at Christ Himself.

We are not simply to be wounded by the law. Allow yourself to be slain by the letter. And allow the Spirit to direct you to the true Source of your Christian life: Jesus

> "We all, with open face beholding as in a glass the glory of the Lord, are changed into the same image from glory to glory, even as by the Spirit of the Lord." (2 Corinthians 3:18)

Suffer fools gladly

"He didn't suffer fools gladly" reads the obituary… "Cantankerous old grouch" we imagine… Or at least I do. I might be wrong in the particulars, but that's how I read the phrase in general.

No-one ever *does* suffer fools gladly. We are only told when someone definitely does *not.* And since, generally, no-one seems to have *any* patience for fools, the person who is *said* 'not to suffer fools gladly' must be very irritable indeed. We can imagine that, in this person's company, it is the fools that do the suffering. And not gladly.

So perhaps we think that the *Christian* response is that *we* should suffer fools gladly. Perhaps this biblical phrase arose as an exhortation to bear with fools with infinite patience.

Well there is something very Christ-like in that practice. Jesus put up with a lot of folly – mainly from His nearest and dearest. We can think of Mark chapter 10 where He has just described the agony and sacrifice of the cross which is before Him (v32-34). Instantly James and John ask Him for glory – they want cabinet posts in the coming kingdom (v35-41). It is such a vulgar and stupid request, especially with the prediction of Golgotha still hanging in the air. If Jesus "didn't suffer fools gladly" we would now get to see James and John put in their place.

But how does Jesus respond? He calls them all together and, with great patience, tells them again of His servant-hearted love (v42-45). *That* is to be their model. Not worldly power-grabs.

Jesus *does* suffer fools gladly. And through His glad-hearted patience He *teaches* fools that they might cease to be fools. How astonishing! Here is the one Man who *does* suffer fools gladly.

But that is not what the Bible exhorts us towards with the phrase "suffer fools gladly." St Paul, who coined the term, does not put himself in the shoes of the patient sufferer. In this phrase, Paul is the fool.

In 2 Corinthians 11, Paul is concerned about the Corinthian church. They are putting up with (i.e. "suffering") the ministry of false apostles (v13). Such false apostles expected generous payments while they boasted of their accomplishments and great giftings. On the other hand Paul expected nothing, nor did he boast about his own service or experiences. But in order to make his point, Paul decides that boasting is the order of the day. Therefore he will make his own boasts to the Corinthians, but they are nothing like the boasts of the false apostles:

> "Seeing that many glory after the flesh, I will glory also. For ye **suffer fools gladly**, seeing ye yourselves are wise. For ye suffer, if a man bring you into bondage, if a man devour you, if a man take of you, if a man exalt himself, if a man smite you on the face."
> (2 Corinthians 11:18-20)

There *are* fools that we should not suffer gladly. They are called false teachers. And we should not tolerate them. Yet Paul says that a curious thing has been happening in Corinth. They have suffered to have slave-drivers among them, bringing them into bondage through their false gospels. Paul is amazed. And so he seeks to shock them out of their complacency by subverting the boasts of the false apostles. He speaks as a fool (v21). In other words he uses the rhetoric of the foolish false teachers, but his message is very different:

> "Are they Hebrews? so am I. Are they Israelites? so am I. Are they the seed of Abraham? so am I. Are they ministers of Christ? (I speak as a fool) I am more; in labours more abundant, in stripes above measure, in prisons more frequent, in deaths oft. Of the Jews five times received I forty stripes save one. Thrice was I beaten with rods, once was I stoned, thrice I suffered shipwreck, a night and a day I have been in the deep; in journeyings often, in perils of waters, in perils of robbers, in perils by mine own countrymen, in perils by the heathen, in perils in the city, in perils in the wilderness, in perils in the sea, in perils among false brethren; In weariness and painfulness, in watchings often, in hunger and thirst, in fastings often, in cold and nakedness. Beside those things that are without, that which cometh upon me daily, the care of all the churches. Who is weak, and I am not weak? who is offended, and I burn not? If I must needs glory, I will glory of the things which concern mine infirmities."
> (2 Corinthians 11:22-30)

Paul's boast is that he is vastly less prosperous, less healthy, less settled and less respectable than all the false teachers they have been entertaining! He boasts in his weakness because *this* is the mark of an authentic follower of Christ.

If Paul is forced into the foolish game of listing his resume, he will "glory of the things which concern [his] infirmities." If the Corinthians suffer those proud fools – the false apostles, Paul hopes they will suffer *him* – a humble fool for Christ.

Today, if someone "doesn't suffer fools gladly", it's usually because they consider themselves to be above the fools. Paul puts himself beneath the fools and begs for the sufferance of the "wise ones"!

In this way he resembles his Lord who could easily have cast away fools like us. Instead Jesus humbles Himself *beneath* our folly – subverting it with His own up-side-down glory. Jesus became a fool on the cross, and His weakness became His glory.

So the question is, Will we be impatient with the folly and weakness of the cross? Or will we suffer *His* kind of folly gladly?

> "We preach Christ crucified, unto the Jews a stumblingblock, and unto the Greeks foolishness; But unto them which are called, both Jews and Greeks, Christ the power of God, and the wisdom of God. Because the foolishness of God is wiser than men; and the weakness of God is stronger than men."
> (1 Corinthians 1:23-25)

30 November – 2 Corinthians 12:1-21

A thorn in my flesh

Difficult people, chronic illness, vocal opposition, disability, bureaucrats in your way – all sorts of long-term problems might be called "a thorn in your flesh."

Ever since the curse was pronounced in Eden, thorns have tormented us:

> "Cursed is the ground for thy sake; in sorrow shalt thou eat of it all the days of thy life; Thorns also and thistles shall it bring forth to thee." (Genesis 3:17-18)

Notice that the thorns are "to thee." Like razor wire pointed at man, the thorns are directed at us. They are designed to make life painful for us. The world is rigged for frustration and the thorns press into our flesh.

In particular, "thorns in your side" is an Old Testament euphemism for foreign enemies (e.g. Numbers 33:55; Judges 2:3). Israel sits among the surrounding nations like a lily among thorns (Song 2:2). True prophets of the LORD are not to be put off by the thorns that encompass them (Ezekiel 2:6), they must continue to hold out the word of the LORD. Unfortunately Israel does not heed those words. Israel itself starts being fruitless and begins to produce thorns (Isaiah 5:1-6). In the end thorns are good for nothing – they will be burned up (Isaiah 9:18; Hebrews 6:8). Yet in the ultimate act of redemption, Christ *wears* thorns as a crown in order to exhaust the curse in Himself. His resurrection future will be a time when thorns and briers are replaced by fruitful trees (Isaiah 55:13).

With this background we come to our phrase for today. Paul is writing 2 Corinthians 12. Here he continues his subversion of the boasting carried on by the false apostles. Where they boasted in their strength, Paul boasts in his weaknesses. Where they recount their fabulous spiritual experiences, Paul is remarkably circumspect about his own.

Yet he does allow himself one oblique reference, here in 2 Corinthians 12. Doubtless Paul refers to himself here, but he distances himself from the experience so much that he recounts it in the third person:

> "I will come to visions and revelations of the Lord. I knew a man in Christ above fourteen years ago, (whether in the body, I cannot tell; or whether out of the body, I cannot tell: God knoweth;) such an one caught up to the third heaven. And I knew such a man, (whether in the body, or out of the body, I cannot tell: God knoweth;) How that he was caught up into paradise, and heard unspeakable words, which it is not lawful for a man to utter. Of such an one will I glory: yet of myself I will not glory, but in mine infirmities. For though I would desire to glory, I shall not be a fool; for I will say the truth: but now I forbear, lest any man should think of me above that which he seeth me to be, or that he heareth of me. And lest I should be exalted above measure through the abundance of the revelations, there was given to me **a thorn in the flesh**, the messenger of Satan to buffet me, lest I should be exalted above measure. For this thing I besought the Lord thrice, that it might depart from me." (2 Corinthians 12:1-8)

Many have speculated about what this thorn might have been for Paul. Perhaps it was a physical infirmity, specifically his eyes (Galatians 4:13-15; cf. Numbers 33:55). Perhaps it was a person or particular sect (note how Scripture describes human enemies as 'thorns in your side' – Judges 2:3; Numbers 33:55). Perhaps it was a particularly strong and enduring spiritual attack (note how Paul calls it 'the messenger of Satan.') But whatever it was, Paul was not able to be free of it. In fact, no matter how he begged Jesus, Jesus would not remove it.

I wonder if our theology of suffering can handle that. Are we able to cope with the fact that, often, Jesus does *not* remove thorns which torment and buffet us?

Sometimes people quote Isaiah 53:5 – "with his stripes we are healed" – and they say 'All healing was purchased at the cross, therefore all healing is available now, we just need to believe for it.' But of course that is faulty theology. It is true that Christ's cross and resurrection purchased all healing. It also purchased a deathless eternity. But we don't enjoy that yet. And Jesus is not committed to prolonging the old world – the cursed creation, doomed in Adam. Jesus is committed to putting that to death and rising up a healed world on the other side of the grave.

Sometime Jesus may choose to heal as a token of that new creation life. But that's not His ultimate commitment for this perishing age. Jesus will not remove all our suffering. And He will not continue to prolong our old lives in these Adamic bodies. Praise God for that! Our hope does not lie in mini-healings and mini-deliverances now. Our hope is not for a present papering-over-the-cracks. Our hope lies in cosmic resurrection when the thorns will be replaced by fir trees (Isaiah 55:13).

In the meantime thorns will buffet us. We should pray, as Paul does, for deliverance from them. Ask, seek and knock for such a healing . But no matter what Christ's answer, here is the heart of His word to you today:

> "My grace is sufficient for thee: for my strength is made perfect in weakness." (2 Corinthians 12:9)

Anyone can bear a miracle to the world as evidence of Christ's grace. Paul bears his suffering to the world. And this is the perfect display of Christ's strength. When *His* grace sustains the sufferer, it is a remarkable show of divine power. Not the power that teleports us out of trouble, but the power that sustains us through it. Christ's strength is a cross-shaped strength.

So Paul concludes…

> "Most gladly therefore will I rather glory in my infirmities, that the power of Christ may rest upon me. Therefore I take pleasure in infirmities, in reproaches, in necessities, in persecutions, in distresses for Christ's sake: for when I am weak, then am I strong." (2 Corinthians 12:9-10)

1 December – Galatians 1:1-10; 2:11-21

Anathema

What do we consider *beyond the pale*? What behaviour or what belief is out of bounds? How does a group or individual prove themselves to be completely unacceptable?

In this context we might say that *so and so* or *such and such* is "anathema."

It might be as trivial as the way a Mac user considers PCs. It might be as serious as the way a pacifist considers torture. But they will label these things "anathema."

It's an untranslated Greek word which literally means, 'something that is placed or set up.' In some circumstances it means a gift – perhaps a sacrificial offering. But in other contexts it means something set apart as *cursed.* That's the meaning it has for us today.

So what do you consider to be "anathema"? What would you guess is the King James Bible's one great "anathema"?

Perhaps we immediately think of behaviours. Perhaps we immediately think of certain heretical doctrines? What is it that the Bible rules out of court so emphatically?

Well look at how the Apostle Paul uses the term:

> "If any man love not the Lord Jesus Christ, let him be Anathema. Maranatha." (1 Corinthians 16:22)

Here are two untranslated words – "Anathema" is Greek, "Maranatha" is Aramaic (it means "Come O Lord"). Between them we see the depths and the heights of his feelings regarding Christ. Paul can think of no greater blasphemy than a loveless heart towards Jesus. And he can think of no greater comfort than the second coming of this Lord who he loves.

When the Lord Jesus *does* come again, there will be one issue which faces the world. None of our many sins will be held against us (2 Corinthians 5:19). We won't be able to hide behind our goodness *or* our badness. It's Christ *Himself* who confronts us and the only question will be "Do you have love for Him who has loved you so extravagantly?"

If we have no love for Jesus we are anathema! The universe was created by Jesus and for Jesus (Colossians 1:16). If we too are not *for* Jesus we are completely out of place. We are violating the very nature of reality. We are cutting against the grain of the cosmos. We do not belong. We are anathema. What place can there be at the Bridegroom's feast for those who do not love the Bridegroom?

This is the one anathema of the King James Bible. (The Greek word is used elsewhere, but here is the only place the Authorised Version leaves it untranslated). Yet the great anathema does not regard bad behaviour or bad belief but a bad heart towards the Lord Jesus. This is the issue for *that* day when the Lord returns. But it's also the issue for *this* day.

We can make life very complicated. Right now, dozens of priorities will be jostling for precedence in your heart. But Paul wants to simplify things for us. Before all else, look to Christ. Before you look to your deeds or your creeds, it's the receiving of Christ *Himself* that matters. Know in your heart that Jesus has loved you and given Himself for you (Galatians 2:20). His posture towards you is arms-wide-open. Do you have *love* for the

Lord Jesus Christ? Look to Him again, today and every day. It is the very stuff of life, now and forever.

2 December – Galatians 6:1-18

A man reaps what he sows

The saying is instantly recognisable as *religious.* Even if few people know where it comes from, most will assume it's biblical. And they'll assume that they know what it means.

It's about cause and effect right? It's saying: 'What goes around, comes around.' 'If you play with fire, you're going to get burned.' 'Everyone gets what they deserve.'

Perhaps we think it's the Bible's version of Karma – a conditional, performance-based spirituality where the books will all balance and justice will have the last word. Therefore, *Look out sinners – a man reaps what he sows.*

But actually Paul's letter to the Galatians (from which our phrase comes) radically subverts this way of thinking.

He begins the letter by pronouncing a deadly anathema on *anyone* who denies or perverts the gospel of grace (Galatians 1:6-9). Even the Apostle Peter gets a blast from Paul when he forgets the truth of our gracious justification (Galatians 2:11-21). Paul is at pains to show that true righteousness has never been won by moral obedience but only by faith alone (Galatians 3-4). It is Christ who earns our salvation through His life, death and resurrection – not us. We are incapable of producing the life of God. The "flesh" we have inherited from Adam (our old nature) cannot work righteousness – though it constantly tries to do so. One of the characteristics of the "flesh" is its desire to self-justify. The flesh loves to live under the law in order to boast in its moral abilities. But no, Christ works righteousness for us, without any assistance from us. Then, wonderfully, we are "clothed in Christ" as the Spirit unites us to Him (Galatians 3:26-4:7).

Therefore a Christian is someone who has their flesh from Adam, but their Spirit from Christ. While the flesh produces Adam-like sin and death, the Spirit bears Christ-like fruit in our lives (Galatians 5).

Therefore Paul exhorts us to live in accordance with the truth. We ought to walk by the Spirit and not by the flesh. That is, we ought to dwell on *Christ's* performance and not our own. We ought to be about Christ's doing and not our own.

In *that* context we come to our verse for today:

> "**Whatsoever a man soweth, that shall he also reap**. For he that soweth to his flesh shall of the flesh reap corruption; but he that soweth to the Spirit shall of the Spirit reap life everlasting." (Galatians 6:7-8)

It turns out that Paul isn't affirming a Christian Karma after all. Actually he's speaking against it. You see the way of the flesh *is* the way of earning, performance and self-glorification. But Paul says – that is a perishing path. To invest in that is to invest in corruption itself. There is an organic union between flesh and death. To sow on this soil reaps exactly what you'd expect.

Yet there is another kind of life. And it's not life 'under the law.' It's not about getting your just deserts. The way of the Spirit is the way of grace. He is always bringing us the things of Christ (John 16:15). To 'sow' to the Spirit is to invest in the gospel word and live by this truth from beyond ourselves. So, again, there is an organic union, this time between the Spirit and life. There's no sense of *reward* or *earning* here, it's just *natural* that dwelling in Christ and He in us will bear good fruit.

A man indeed reaps what he sows. But this is not the law of 'just deserts', this is the truth of undeserved mercy. Stop sowing to the way of Adam, the way of flesh, the way of boasting, the way of performance, the way of law. That life is over for you. Only corruption can be reaped there. Instead, allow the Spirit draw you into the unshakeable love of the Father and Son:

> "God hath sent forth the Spirit of his Son into your hearts, crying, Abba, Father." (Galatians 4:6)

This is the truth of our position – filled with the Spirit, united to the Son, calling on the Father. Receive that sure reality by faith and you are sowing on *very* fertile ground.

3 December – Ephesians 3:1-21

The unsearchable riches of Christ

What is the message of Christianity for the world? If you could boil it down, what is the proclamation of the church? Paul has a wonderful summary in Ephesians 3:8.

John Wycliffe translated it: "the vnserchable richessis of Crist".

William Tyndale put it as: "the unsearchable ryches of Christ."

And, in that tradition, the King James Bible rendered the verse like this:

> "Unto me, who am less than the least of all saints, is this grace given, that I should preach among the Gentiles **the unsearchable riches of Christ**."

This is the subject of Paul's preaching: "Christ's riches."

He uses the word "riches" six times in Ephesians (1:7,18; 2:4,7; 3:8,16). It's the word that describes Abraham's wealth (Genesis 13:2), and Solomon's (1 Kings 3:13), and 'the rich man's' (Mark 10:25). Yet Christ's abundance far surpasses these "rich men." It is "unsearchable."

How do we feel about the super-rich? Envy? Contempt? Fear? Well Christ has "unsearchable riches". He's not just "the 1%," He's the 0.000000000000001%. What do we feel about His fabulous wealth?

Actually Paul feels brim full of joy and gratitude. Because these riches are riches of grace and mercy. Christ is not only stinking rich, He is a profligate philanthropist, as we shall see.

Let's trace through Paul's use of "riches" in Ephesians.

We begin before the foundation of the world with Christ, the Father's heavenly storehouse (Ephesians 1:3). From eternity He commits all things into the Son's hands (John 3:35). The nations are His inheritance (Psalm 2:8). The whole creation is a love gift for Him (Colossians 1:15-16). Christ has unsearchable riches because He is the Father's Firstborn, the Heir Apparent, the Beloved Son. But just as these riches flow from Father to Son, so they overflow from Christ to the world. Such riches are a super-abundance of divine love and generosity, and so…

> "God, who is **rich** in mercy, for his great love wherewith he loved us, even when we were dead in sins, hath quickened us together with Christ, (by grace ye are saved)." (Ephesians 2:4-5)

God's riches are riches *of mercy*. And they are lavished on we, the dirt poor. We weren't just "in the gutter" we had "bitten the dust" – dead in sins. Yet the Father's fabulous wealth is employed in raising us up with Christ. This wealth is expended in a costly "redemption"…

> "In [Christ] we have redemption through his blood, the forgiveness of sins, according to the **riches** of his grace; Wherein he hath abounded toward us in all wisdom and prudence;" (Ephesians 1:7-8)

These divine riches are not drawn down without cost. The astonishing mercy of Christ is purchased with His own blood. Yet, in His grace, He pays this ultimate price for our freedom and forgiveness.

Now we stand as witnesses to heaven and earth of our generous Father:

> "God hath raised us up together, and made us sit together in heavenly places in Christ Jesus: That in the ages to come he might shew the exceeding **riches** of his grace in his kindness toward us through Christ Jesus." (Ephesians 2:6-7)

God is rich and will be known as rich.

But perhaps you don't feel able to appreciate this wealth. Maybe you're not feeling the benefits of this incredible union with Christ? Well God's riches don't just bestow grace, they also enable you to *appreciate* such grace:

> "[I pray that the Father] would grant you, according to the **riches** of his glory, to be strengthened with might by his Spirit in the inner man; That Christ may dwell in your hearts by faith." (Ephesians 3:16-17)

Here is a wonderful truth: God even has riches that awaken us to the riches that He's already bestowed! Talk about grace upon grace.

So God's present riches make us appreciate His past riches. But, more than this, Paul prays we would know His future riches too…

> "[I pray] that ye may know… the **riches** of the glory of his inheritance in the saints." (Ephesians 1:18)

What a day of sumptuous opulence! What overwhelming prosperity we will enjoy when we are heirs of God and co-heirs with Christ of the whole cosmos. To cap it all off, that day will be the day that the Lord inherits *us,* His saints. How incredible – the riches that will flow when Christ returns!

What can we do in the meantime except…

> "…to preach among the *nations* the unsearchable riches of Christ." (Ephesians 3:8)

Christ is the storehouse of the Father's overflowing bounty. We are beggars, more than destitute in our sins. Yet, through Christ, we have been adopted as heirs into that eternal royal Family.

We call on an "Abba, Father" who is mind-blowingly rich and who, literally, loves us to death! Does that change the way you approach your day today?

Maybe your earthly father had short arms and deep pockets. Or long arms and shallow pockets. Or crossed arms and closed pockets.

Your Father in heaven is different. In Jesus we have come to a Father who is both super-wealthy and over-flowingly kind. So rejoice in your generous God. And preach to the world "the unsearchable riches of Christ."

4 December – Ephesians 4:1-32

Let not the sun go down upon your wrath

In his wonderful book on Ephesians, Watchman Nee observes that the letter can be divided into three movements: "Sit, Walk, Stand."

> We are *seated* in the heavenly places in Christ Jesus. (Eph 2:6)
>
> We then *walk* worthy of our calling in Christ. (Eph 4:1)
>
> And we *stand* against the assaults of the evil one. (Eph 6:10-17)

The order is important. *First* we learn our true position in Christ – raised, forgiven, adopted, beloved and inheriting the cosmos. *Then* we learn how to walk out into the world on that basis. *Finally* we learn how to stand against Satan's attacks, knowing that we already hold the high ground.

As far as Nee was concerned, all our problems in the Christian life stem from a failure to appreciate our *seatedness*. When we try to *walk* before we have *sat*, we fall down! We imagine that Christianity consists of performing certain duties or cultivating certain characteristics. Yet our new life really *has* been given to us in Jesus.

Thus, as he turns from "Sit" (Ephesians 1-3) to "Walk" (Ephesians 4-5) Nee makes this comment:

> "God has given us Christ. There is nothing now for us to receive outside of Him. The Holy Spirit has been sent to produce what is of Christ in us; not to produce anything that is apart from or outside of Him…We have been accustomed to look upon holiness as a virtue, upon humility as a grace, upon love as a gift to be sought from God. But the Christ of God is *Himself* everything that we shall ever need… Our life *is* the life of Christ, mediated in us by the indwelling Holy Spirit Himself."

Given that this is so, the very first area of our "walk" which Paul addresses is the realm of "words" (Ephesians 4:1-25). In the word, Christ is given to us again by the Spirit. Therefore the body of Christ is a word-full body. We are forever returning to the gospel word to tell us of our true position – seated at God's right hand. In spite of all worldly evidence to the contrary, we walk by faith not by sight. In other words, we "walk" by the "word". Thus we are constantly "speaking the truth in love [that we] may grow up into him in all things." (Ephesians 4:15)

As Paul considers this, he raises the issue of words that go wrong. In verse 29 he will talk about "corrupt communication." In verse 31 he exhorts us to put away "evil speaking". But in verse 26 he writes our fascinating little verse:

> "Be ye angry, and sin not: **let not the sun go down upon your wrath**." (Ephesians 4:26)

Paul is aware that anger is a reality in our daily communication. If we're not tempted to daily anger, perhaps we are not walking with our brothers and sisters in close enough communion!

Anger arises when our desires are thwarted (James 4:1-3). Most often our desires are inappropriate, but sometimes our desires are good and proper and therefore their frustration involves a righteous anger. In such situations we are to "be angry and not sin." The anger is not to be suppressed but addressed. And addressed quickly.

In the Bible, days end at sunset because each day is a microcosm (a little world). Each day begins in darkness (at dusk), but the light triumphs over the darkness. If that is the story of the world, then it must be the story of our lives. Darkness must not have the last word in our relationships. We must end with the light of grace and reconciliation.

Therefore Paul exhorts us to sort out our quarrels before the day is out. In *this* way we will be imitators of God. *His* final word to the world is not wrath but mercy. Notice how Paul grounds all our human acts of reconciliation in God's great reconciliation in Christ.

> "Be ye kind one to another, tenderhearted, forgiving one another, even as God for Christ's sake hath forgiven you. Be ye therefore followers of God, as dear children; And walk in love, as Christ also hath loved us, and hath given himself for us." (Ephesians 4:32-5:2)

Sit in that truth – Christ has loved us and given Himself for us. We *are* at peace with the living God, though it cost Him everything to secure it. Now walk by that light.

Are there people you need to reconcile with? "Let not the sun go down upon your wrath."

Likeminded

William Tyndale gave us the word, "likeminded", but what gives us the reality?

On the internet it's easy to find "people like us". No matter how specialist our interests might be, the online world is so large, any subgroup at all can find "likeminded" members.

But what about in the local church? What about in face to face community where people of all ages, races and cultures are called together by the Spirit? How can we find unity there?

That was a big concern for Paul in his letter to the Philippians. There were high profile spats within the congregation and it was affecting the witness of the church. Therefore Paul urges these Christians:

> "… be **likeminded**, having the same love, being of one accord, of one mind. Let nothing be done through strife or vainglory; but in lowliness of mind let each esteem other better than themselves." (Philippians 2:2-3)

Notice how important singleness of mind is to Paul. But how will it come about?

Well the answer, as always, is in Jesus. Paul writes in verse 5:

> "Let this mind be in you, which was also in Christ Jesus:"

The *mind* we are to be *like* is Christ's. And what is the mind of Christ? Well in the following verses, Paul either writes or quotes from a stunning hymn that reveals the eternal thought-life of the Son of God:

> "Who, being in the form of God, thought it not robbery to be equal with God: But made himself of no reputation, and took upon him the form of a servant, and was made in the likeness of men: And being found in fashion as a man, he humbled himself, and became obedient unto death, even the death of the cross." (Philippians 2:6-8)

You and I did not choose to be born. The eternal Christ did! He made up His *mind* to take flesh. This is incredible. Because if I ever *did* have the choice to be born, I would not have chosen what Jesus chose. If I was in the form of God, surrounded by the worship of heaven, in the direct presence of my Father, I would not have chosen the birth, life and death which the Son of God determined for Himself. Jesus chose a life of "no reputation", of service (slavery even), humility, obedience and death – even the godforsaken death of the cross.

When we see the baby in the manger, it's like watching a man falling. He has come from the highest heights. And on Christmas morning we see Him heading down, down, down, from heaven to earth, and eventually to hell on that cross.

And all of this happens because Jesus made up His *mind* to serve. Being in the form of God He has a *mind* to serve. And – this is crucial to understand – such service was not a departure from the divine glory, it is the very expression of it. The true Godness of God is shown when Christ climbs down off the throne and pours Himself out as a servant. Wriggling in the manger, writhing on the cross – there is the expression of true deity. And when the Father sees His Son pouring Himself out in service…

> "Wherefore God also hath highly exalted him, and given him a name which is above every name: That at the name of Jesus every knee should bow, of things in heaven, and things in earth, and things under the earth; And that every tongue should confess that Jesus Christ is Lord, to the glory of God the Father." (Philippians 2:9-11)

Because of the crib and the cross, *therefore* the Father says "Have the crown!" What is crowned *is* the self-emptying love of the crib and the cross. The Father vindicates suffering love as the true display of divine glory. He vindicates the suffering Servant as the true LORD of heaven and earth.

And one day everyone will bow the knee to Jesus, the LORD. They will do so ***because*** He poured out His life to death.

> "Worthy is the Lamb that was slain to receive power, and riches, and wisdom, and strength, and honour, and glory, and blessing." (Revelation 5:12)

One day the whole world will recognise what the Father has declared in exalting Jesus to His right hand: The sacrificial Servant is LORD. Humble, self-abandoning love is enthroned as the very heart-beat of deity. The mind of the Servant is the mind of God.

And so Paul says: "Be likeminded… let this mind be in you which was also in Christ Jesus." (Philippians 2:2,5)

We are a fractious bunch, we humans. But here's the solution. The Christian has their thinking completely reoriented by the mind of Christ. Humility is greatness, service is glory, but sacrifice is divine. When we really think like that we will esteem each other better than ourselves.

You see the saying from today's picture is wrong. Or at least it needs recalibrating by the gospel of Christ. But the reality is this: *Humble* minds think alike.

6 December – Philippians 3:1-4:9

Passeth all understanding

We can often feel besieged by worries. Demands seem to threaten us from every side. We dare not step out into our calling lest we be crushed by pressures too great for us.

Some of us respond by shutting down. "There is a lion without, I shall be slain in the streets" we cry, bolting the door against such dangers (Proverbs 22:13). Others of us raise a war cry and run into battle, confident of our own powers. Paul has a different approach.

He says "Be careful for nothing."

In the Greek, it's the exact same phrase as Jesus' repeated command of Matthew 6: "Take no thought". It means "Don't have many and divided thoughts." Easier said than done. When we're besieged by worries our minds run in a thousand directions at once. But Paul (and Jesus) counsel us to stop: "Be careful for *nothing*." It's an all-embracing negative. And it's followed by an all-inclusive positive: "In *everything* by prayer and supplication with thanksgiving let your requests be made known unto God."

Paul doesn't tell us to squash our many fears. Instead he invites us to view them as "requests". Did you realise that all of your worries are actually requests? Requests which so often go unexpressed. Requests which God Himself is eager to hear.

What does this assume about ourselves and about God?

First, it assumes that we're not very good at discerning our many desires… let alone expressing them… let alone addressing them to *God.* But, second, it assumes that we have a God who is *intimately* concerned for our many troubles. As the Lord's Prayer teaches us, we have a Father who is not only interested in His kingdom coming but also in our daily bread.

Therefore, of *course* we pray "with thanksgiving." We are grateful for a Father so kind and so powerful that He attends to our every supplication.

The little phrase "with thanksgiving" is so easily forgotten. But there can be no peace if we simply bring our shopping lists to God. Without an awareness of the grace of our Father and an attendant gratitude, all our petitioning is liable to heighten our fears, not allay them. But with faith in a generous Father, Paul attaches this promise to our prayers…

> "the peace of God, which **passeth all understanding**, shall keep your hearts and minds through Christ Jesus."

Here is something unknown to the world. Not just stress management but a peace that "**passeth all understanding**." No mere trick of the mind can deliver what Paul offers here. There can be no earthly explanation of *this* peace. It's beyond our wit and wisdom. Because this is a peace that wages war on our fears.

What do I mean? Well the word for "keep" is very strong. Paul uses it in two other places. In 2 Corinthians he uses it to describe a garrison of soldiers guarding a city (2 Corinthians 11:32). In Galatians 3, he speaks of the saints of old "shut up" under the Mosaic law (Galatians 3:23). It's a word that means "hold prisoner" or "besiege."

So this is the reversal of our fears. Right now you may feel besieged by worries. But there is a cavalry. There is a greater force to call on. "Through Christ Jesus" you have perfect access to a generous Father. So then, turn your problems to prayers and know: it's His peace that besieges you.

7 December – Colossians 3:1-17

Bowels of mercy

Anyone who's really loved (or feared) knows that the *heart* is not the only emotional organ. Some of our greatest loves and our greatest fears are felt a little further south – in the guts!

So while we might be used to speaking of a sinking heart, the Scriptures are comfortable speaking of churning bowels!

> **Genesis 43:30** "And Joseph made haste; for his bowels did yearn upon his brother [Benjamin]"
>
> **Song of Solomon 5:4** "My beloved put in his hand by the hole of the door, and my bowels were moved for him."
>
> **Jeremiah 4:19** "[The LORD says] My bowels, my bowels! I am pained at my very heart; my heart maketh a noise in me;"

> **Lamentations 1:20** "Behold, O LORD; for I am in distress: my bowels are troubled"

We speak of gut-wrenching emotions. The King James Bible, in faithfulness to the underlying Hebrew and Greek, just takes that language one step further. And notice that all of these visceral reactions are right and good responses to the situation. You might call them healthy bowel movements. On the other hand, a lack of compassion is considered to be a nasty bowel complaint. So to the loveless Corinthians Paul writes:

> "ye are straitened in your own bowels." (2 Corinthians 6:12)

And John describes a loveless Christian who has "shutteth up his bowels of compassion." (1 John 3:17).

Therefore there is great need for our sluggish bowels to be "refreshed." Apparently Philemon was particularly good at this:

> "For we have great joy and consolation in thy love, because the bowels of the saints are refreshed by thee, brother." (Philemon 1:7)

> "Yea, brother, let me have joy of thee in the Lord: refresh my bowels in the Lord." (Philemon 1:20)

What would it mean to be refreshed in this way? Well Paul speaks of a change that has already happened to the Christian. It's foundational to our emotional renewal.

> "Put on therefore, as the elect of God, holy and beloved, bowels of mercies, kindness, humbleness of mind, meekness, longsuffering;" (Colossians 3:12)

The Christian *is* elect of God (that is, chosen – *choice* in the Father's eyes). The Christian *is* holy (that is, special – set apart as His own). The Christian *is* beloved (that is, a child of the King and dearly loved).

Notice in all these things that Christians *are* what Christ **is**. Christ is the original and eternal Elect One. Christ is the original and eternal Holy One. Christ is the original and eternal Beloved Son. And, by faith, we come to share in His status and life.

Therefore, says Paul, since we are such a people, let us put on *His* bowels of mercies. Here is one more way we will share in Christ's life – to share in His stomach-churning love. You see it is *Christ* who loves with a visceral, gut-wrenching passion.

Let me explain. There is a verb form of the Greek word for "bowels". It means, most basically, *to be moved in ones bowels*, but the KJV translates it more idiomatically as "moved with compassion." This word is used only in the Gospels and only to describe the emotional life of Jesus.

> **Matthew 9:36** "But when he saw the multitudes, he was moved with compassion on them…"
>
> **Matthew 14:14** "And Jesus went forth, and saw a great multitude, and was moved with compassion toward them…"
>
> **Matthew 15:32** "Then Jesus called his disciples unto him, and said, I have compassion on the multitude…"
>
> **Matthew 20:34** "So Jesus had compassion on [the two blind men], and touched their eyes…"
>
> **Mark 1:41** "And Jesus, moved with compassion, put forth his hand, and touched [the leper]…"
>
> **Luke 7:13** "And when the Lord saw [the widow], he had compassion on her…"

In addition to these Gospel accounts there are three characters in Christ's parables that are said to be moved with compassion: The King of the Unmerciful Servant, The Good Samaritan and The Father of the Prodigal Son. We've seen previously how each of these are a pictures of Christ Himself. It is *Christ's* character to be moved with pity in His innermost parts. Churned up inside. Profoundly stirred towards mercy and love.

And not only does Christ share with us His standing before the Father, He shares with us His "bowels of mercies." When we love our brothers and sisters we are participating in Christ's love for them. We are "moved with compassion" in the name of Jesus. That's why Paul is able to say that he longs after the Philippians "in the bowels of Jesus Christ." (Philippians 1:8) Paul loves with the very love of Jesus.

So please don't think me rude, I'm only being biblical, but how are your bowel movements? You know what I mean. Are your bowels of mercies straitened and shut up? Or are you moved with compassion?

Return to the Lord Jesus by faith. See *His* compassion – perhaps read one of the Gospel stories from the quotes above. Allow yourself to be moved once again. As a chosen, holy and beloved child of God, Christ's compassion *is* yours.

8 December – 1 Thessalonians 1:1-9

Labour of love

The Christian life is one of waiting and of working.

Advent puts us in mind of the waiting. We look not only to Christ's first coming, but ahead to His second coming, to judge the living and the dead.

Here is how Old Testament saints waited for that first coming:

> "I wait for the LORD, my soul doth wait, and in his word do I hope. My soul waiteth for the Lord more than they that watch for the morning: I say, more than they that watch for the morning. Let Israel hope in the LORD: for with the LORD there is mercy, and with him is plenteous redemption. 8 And he shall redeem Israel from all his iniquities." (Psalm 130:5-8)

The long-awaited Lord did indeed come to redeem Israel from all their iniquities. But His first coming does not do away with waiting.

Paul explains this in 1 Thessalonians chapter 1 (the passage from which our phrase originates). He narrates the conversion story of the Thessalonians:

> "Ye turned to God from idols to serve the living and true God; And to wait for his Son from heaven, whom he raised from the dead, even Jesus, which delivered us from the wrath to come." (1 Thessalonians 1:9-10)

The Christian *waits* for Christ to come again. We don't wait nervously for 'Judgement Day', unsure of the outcome. No, through His first coming Christ delivered us from the coming wrath. We wait confidently as those who love Him and long to see Him face to face.

When I was engaged to my wife we were on opposite sides of the planet. In fact our relationship was 'long-distance' for over a year. But here's what kept me faithful to her – and more than that, here's what kept our long-distance relationship positively vibrant: We were waiting for our wedding day. And that expectancy shaped virtually every minute of our lives. Simply waiting for this future rendered any notions of infidelity unthinkable. Waiting was *not* an absence of activity. It wasn't a *lack* that needed filling. It was not a nothing preceding a something. It was a something of enormous substance. Waiting in this sense is a tangible reality.

So it is with the Christian. We wait to see Jesus.

But how do we wait? Like the picture above? Scanning the sky for signs of His coming? Scouring the newspapers for clues to His advent?

We're called to be on the welcoming committee, but many want to be in the planning group. It's something Jesus refuses to bring us in on. Just before He ascended His followers wanted to get an eschatological timetable from Him:

> "When they therefore were come together, they asked of him, saying, Lord, wilt thou at this time restore again the kingdom to Israel? And he said unto them, It is not for you to know the times or the seasons, which the Father hath put in his own power. But ye shall receive power, after that the Holy Ghost is come upon you: and ye shall be witnesses unto me both in Jerusalem, and in all Judaea, and in Samaria, and unto the uttermost part of the earth." (Acts 1:6-8)

They wanted to know times and seasons. Jesus says 'That's not your job! Your job is to be witnesses to the ends of the earth.'

We do not wait by worrying about *when*. We wait by witnessing.

It's interesting how Acts 1 continues. Jesus ascends to heaven, the disciples are – understandably, you'd think – gazing into the heavens. But angels appear to tell them to stop gawping at the skies (Acts 1:10-11). The posture of the church, as we wait for Christ, is not stationary, faces heavenwards. Instead our posture is shaped by Acts 1:8 – we've been given our marching orders and out we go – to the ends of the earth as witnesses of Christ.

And so in the same chapter that tells us of the Thessalonians "waiting for God's Son from heaven" Paul also gives us this description of their current life:

> "[We remember] without ceasing your work of faith, and **labour of love**, and patience of hope in our Lord Jesus Christ." (1 Thessalonians 1:3)

Here again is Paul's famous trio: faith, hope and love. Our faith looks back to Christ's first coming and it inspires work. Our hope looks forward to Christ's second coming and brings patience. And love is the atmosphere of our present lives – confident of the salvation Christ *has* won, and expectant of the cosmic redemption He *will* bring. Now we are free from having to build our own identity or secure our own future. Now we can love. And this love will be a busy, active thing. It is a "*labour* of love."

We're not working *towards* our vindication, our joy, our purpose in life. We're working *from* that sure gift from Christ. Therefore Christian work is a "labour of *love*."

Are your Christian efforts "a labour of love"? If they're feeling more of a "millstone around your neck", then these aren't the kind of labours that will honour Jesus. Let me suggest that you may have forgotten the other two elements of the trio. Remember, we have a sure *faith*, grounded in Christ's first coming. And we have a certain *hope*, expectant of His second coming. If you want to rekindle the love: look again to Christ this Advent – His faultless work for you and your expectant wait for Him. A fresh vision of Jesus turns labour into "a labour of *love*."

9 December – 1 Timothy 6:1-12

Money is the root of all evil

Here's a verse of the bible which everyone knows. Except that they don't.

1 Timothy 6:10 does not say "Money is the root of all evil." It says "the *love* of money is the root of all evil." And if we really wanted to pick up on the nuances in the Greek, we would render it: "the love of money is *a* root of *all kinds of* evil."

Not quite as snappy though is it? Which is why the blunt version has survived. It has the advantage of being comprehensive, memorable and sensational. It gets dropped in conversations as an epitaph when the banker is busted for fraud. "Ah, just goes to show, money is the root of all evil."

The (mis)quote was commonly placarded at the Occupy movements last year. When I spoke to protestors at St Paul's I was surprised by how often the phrase was mentioned. In fact I was surprised in general at how many spoke in biblical terms. (And, by the way, their translation of choice seemed to be the good ol' King James!)

As a placard it's pleasingly reductionist. If we're looking for radical solutions (remember "radical" means going to the "root") then money is an obvious target. It's simple then to focus on the financial system as the source of our woes – and, hey, biblical support just adds weight. For some anyway.

But it was interesting when I spoke to one protestor about the verse. I said to him, "Do you know that the verse doesn't say "money is the root of all evil"?" "No?" he asked. "No, it says "the *love* of money is the root of all evil. And you can love money whether you're rich or poor can't you?"

This hit home with him. We'd just been chatting about the "fat cat bankers" who walked past St Paul's every day. He'd been wistfully spinning a tale of these bankers' imagined lifestyles. The protestor was unemployed, living in a tent, but he realised he was just as capable of a *love* of money as any pin-striped City worker.

He'd been plotting the demise of the global financial system. He'd been speaking of "expropriating" the wealth of the 1% to build a better world. But what if "money" wasn't exactly the problem? What if the "love" of money was the radical evil at the heart of us all?

There's no 'new world order' that can get to the heart. No fat cat tax can fix the affections. If we're looking for "roots" we need to go deeper than money. We must get to the heart.

Don't get me wrong, money can be a deadly trap. As Paul has just said:

> "They that will be rich fall into temptation and a snare, and into many foolish and hurtful lusts, which drown men in destruction and perdition." (1 Timothy 6:9)

Such strong language. And just after our phrase, Paul says:

Some coveted after [money, and]… have erred from the faith, and pierced themselves through with many sorrows.

Money is *incredibly* dangerous. Just consider some of the phrases Jesus Himself gave us:

> Where your treasure is, there your heart will be also
>
> Ye cannot serve God and Mammon
>
> A man's life does not consist in the abundance of his possessions
>
> Camel through the eye of a needle

Money has every chance of becoming a competing god in our lives. In Paul's language, it's something that can "tempt", "ensnare", enflame "lust" and make us "covet". But money itself is not the problem. It's the *love* of money that is *so* dangerous.

Which is why Paul's revolutionary teaching on riches does not focus on redistribution. Instead he rounds off the chapter like this:

> Charge them that are rich in this world, that they be not highminded, nor trust in uncertain riches, but in the living God, who giveth us richly all things to enjoy; That they do good, that they be rich in good works, ready to distribute, willing to communicate; Laying up in store for themselves a good foundation against the time to come, that they may lay hold on eternal life. (1 Timothy 6:17-19)

Sharing the wealth is part of what Paul charges. But that's only part. Notice the true riches Paul directs us to? The living God gives us ***richly*** all things to enjoy. Money promises to give us… freedom, comfort, protection, provision. But money can't really deliver on those things. And if we trust in "uncertain riches" they will prove a snare.

Instead, look to the unsearchable riches of Christ, who is given to us so freely and so fully. He is Heir of the cosmos and shares all things generously with us. One day – in "the time to come" – He will show us our inheritance here on the renewed earth and it will take our breath away. In the words of Isaiah we will see the King in His beauty and a land that stretches afar (Isaiah 33:17).

How can money hold a candle to *Christ?*

10 December – 2 Timothy 3:14-4:5

Itching ears

One of the most pervasive myths of the modern world is this: We think we know what we want. We think we know what's best for us. And we think we ourselves are the best judges of these matters.

The truth could not be further from this common misconception.

In the book of Proverbs, **Wisdom** speaks a frightening truth:

> "All they that hate me love death." (Proverbs 8:36)

The natural state of the human heart is to be estranged from Christ our Wisdom. And in that perverse condition our desires are completely twisted. We hate the Fountain of Living Waters and we love the pit of curses and death.

Therefore what do we look for in our moral and spiritual guides? The truth? Never. Not naturally. Instead we look for leaders who will tell us what we want to hear.

Notice how Jesus put it: "Because I tell you the truth, ye believe me not." (John 8:45)

Jesus doesn't say '*In spite of* my truth telling you don't believe.' He says '*Because* of my truth-telling you don't believe.' We are not naturally oriented to truth. We flee it when it's spoken. Instead we 'turn to fables' as the Apostle Paul put it so memorably:

> For the time will come when they will not endure sound doctrine; but after their own lusts shall they heap to themselves teachers, having **itching ears**; And they shall turn away their ears from the truth, and shall be turned unto fables. (2 Timothy 4:3-4)

An "itching ear" is such an evocative phrase. Itches aren't just satisfied by scratching – they demand to be scratched. They only seem to increase if they go un-heeded. Paul says our ears are like this. We don't merely *like* to hear pleasant lies, we demand to hear them. And Paul says there's always a ready supply of phoney prophets who will scratch us where we itch. It's not just a problem for the last days. The prophet Isaiah spoke of the same reality 8 centuries earlier:

> This is a rebellious people, lying children, children that will not hear the law of the LORD: Which say to the seers, "See not;" and to the prophets, "Prophesy not unto us right things, speak unto us smooth things, prophesy deceits: Get you out of the way, turn aside out of the path, cause the Holy One of Israel to cease from before us." (Isaiah 30:9-11)

I don't think Isaiah is imagining that the people are articulating these words. I'm not sure any Israelite was literally saying "speak unto us smooth things, prophesy deceits." It's just that they would not put up with God's word, they reacted angrily to the truth of the gospel but warmly to the "smooth things." At an unspoken level they had struck a deal with the false prophets – "Tell us what we want to hear, and we'll give you an eager audience." In every age people have found such a deal attractive.

Therefore we must question this myth of the modern world. We do not know what is good for us. As the Proverb says "Counsel in the heart of man is like deep water; but a man of understanding will draw it out." (Proverbs 20:5). We don't know ourselves very well. We don't know what we need. We need The Man of understanding to tell us the truth. We need truth to come to us from the outside. The kind of truth we would never conceive ourselves.

The truth that says we are utterly lost and damned in ourselves but completely loved and redeemed in Jesus. The truth that leaves our own desires and schemes out of the equation but takes up our cause anyway. The truth that puts us to death on the cross and raises us up in resurrection.

Don't trust your natural itches. Don't pursue the lies that puff you up. Listen to the truth from beyond. It will burst your bubble but, then, it will give you a hope you could never have dreamt of. The truth from which we flee is the most extreme but wonderful news in the world. It's far worse than we'd ever feared – but far greater than we'd ever imagined.

11 December – 2 Timothy 2:1-7; 4:6-8

Fight the good fight

In the space of one verse Paul gives us three phrases:

> "I have fought a good fight, I have finished my course, I have kept the faith." (2 Timothy 4:7)

"Fighting the good fight", "finishing the course" and "keeping the faith" have all become well-known. Perhaps this trifecta of famous phrases is not surprising since Paul meant it to be memorable.

This is the last chapter of the last letter he wrote. Tradition has it Paul was beheaded in Rome in AD67 and here is the epitaph he chooses for himself. He's a fighter, a runner, a perseverer. As he approaches the end of his life he inspires *us* towards the same.

Paul is writing to his spiritual son Timothy, passing on the baton of gospel work. Crucially, Paul was the last of a dying breed. He had met with the risen Christ and been an eye-witness of His glory. Soon there would be no-one left on earth who could say that.

So as the church's last foundational apostle, how does Paul encourage the next generation? Chapter 2 gives a sense of his burden.

> Thou therefore, my son, be strong in the grace that is in Christ Jesus. And the things that thou hast heard of me among many witnesses, the same commit thou to faithful men, who shall be able to teach others also. Thou therefore endure hardness, as a good soldier of Jesus Christ. No man that warreth entangleth himself with the affairs of this life; that he may please him who hath chosen him to be a soldier. And if a man also strive for masteries, yet is he not crowned, except he strive lawfully. The husbandman that laboureth must be first partaker of the fruits. Consider what I say; and the Lord give thee understanding in all things. (2 Timothy 2:1-7)

Paul knows that his eye-witness testimony will *not* die out with him. In verse 2 he envisions four generations of gospel ministry. From Paul to Timothy to Timothy's trainees to their trainees. On and on it goes until it reaches you and me.

But, of course, it doesn't stop with us. We too will commit this gospel message to others. And they to others, and so on. The saying is true: "God's grace always runs downhill." It applies to proclamation too. In fact grace and proclamation are almost synonyms.

From Christ's exaltation and the Pentecostal outpouring, there has been a gospel flow which has reached even us. Now we are caught up in its movement.

As I say this, though, I might be conjuring up the wrong kind of imagery – fountains and babbling brooks and floating along. Paul's imagery is much more robust. How does it feel to be gripped by this gospel and pass it on? Like a soldier, like an athlete, like a farmer.

Today let's think about the soldier: enduring, obedient, single-minded. For a soldier, all of life is channelled into the task in hand. There might long periods when the soldier is not "at the front", but they are always battle-ready.

At the end of it all, though, there is a goal. Beyond the discipline and gruelling hard-work there is victory.

As Paul ends his final letter, this is where his mind goes – the end of his "good fight." Thus it completes an image he initiated with his first letter:

> Thanks be to God, which giveth us the victory through our Lord Jesus Christ. (1 Corinthians 15:57)

From the outset, the victory *is* given. But there's still a fight and it lasts till the day we die. One day, though, the fight will be *fought.* Peace will reign and all of Christ's soldiers will rest.

12 December – 2 Timothy 4:6-8; 1 Corinthians 9:19-27

Finish the course

We've been thinking about Paul's parting words to Timothy:

> I have fought a good fight, I have finished my course, I have kept the faith. (2 Timothy 4:7)

First Paul compares himself to a single-minded soldier. The victory is certain in Jesus but the fight remains arduous. One day, however, it will be finished and peace will reign.

Now we turn to the imagery of an athlete. The "course" which Paul pictures is a running track. And the Christian is an athlete – compelled by a vision of the crown and striving to persevere to the end.

Athletes make immense sacrifices to compete in the games. But a vision of Olympic glory sustains them through long-hours of training and many set-backs. Paul wants to instil this basic long-termism in Timothy. After the exhaustion and self-sacrifice comes the prize. And the prize is worth it.

That's how he goes on…

> Henceforth there is laid up for me a crown of righteousness, which the Lord, the righteous judge, shall give me at that day: and

> not to me only, but unto all them also that love his appearing. (2 Timothy 4:8)

In our modern games the athletes are awarded medals. In the ancient games it was a crown.

Who is the crown for? Well Paul's phrasing is telling. He does not say "This crown is for all who have soldiered as hard as I have." He does not say "This victory is for all who have run as hard as I have." He does not say "This crown is for all who have persevered as valiantly as I have." No, the crown is for those who "love his appearing."

If we simply love Jesus. If we simply want *Him* - then we will receive the crown.

What kind of crown is Paul anticipating? Well he tells us in Philippians and 1 Thessalonians. He calls them:

> my brethren, dearly beloved and longed for, my joy and crown (Philippians 4:1)

> What is our hope, or joy, or crown of rejoicing? Are not even ye in the presence of our Lord Jesus Christ at his coming? For ye are our glory and joy. (1 Thessalonians 2:19-20)

Paul's crown will be to share in the victory of Christ *with* the Philippians, *with* the Thessalonians, *with* Timothy. That's the prize which makes all our efforts worthwhile: we will enjoy Christ along with all those we have touched with His love.

Think now of those you've ministered to in the name of Jesus? Think of those you *want* to see sharing in Christ's future feast? They are your crown.

Stay the course. It's definitely worth it.

13 December – 2 Timothy 4:6-8; James 5:7-12

Keep the faith

At the end of your days, what would you like to say? How would you want to summarize your life?

Facing death, Paul was able to say he's "fought the good fight", he's "stayed the course" and he's "kept the faith" (2 Timothy 4:7).

We've seen how these three phrases parallel the images of Christian service he gave in chapter 2. Christians are like soldiers, like athletes and like farmers.

As a soldier, he's "fought", as an athlete, he's "finished", as a farmer, he's "kept". You see in Bible terms, farmers "keep" their land and their livestock (see for instance Genesis 2:15). And Paul says the life of faith is like farming: an arduous, unglamorous life of perseverance.

But it's not all hard-work. There's also reward along the way...

> The husbandman that laboureth must be first partaker of the fruits. (2 Timothy 2:6)

Farmers get to eat their own food and Christian workers get to enjoy the fruits of their labours too. In the New Testament, this fruit is understood as those who come to faith (e.g. Romans 15:16; James 1:18).

This is what sustains the hard-working Christian. In all our labours there are the encouragements of new life and fruitfulness in the gospel. But the real goal is at the end. When Christ returns there is a glorious harvest. So Paul would say to us, enjoy the firstfruits and keep going: the final harvest will be glorious.

So then, as you long for Christ's appearing, as you pass on His gospel hope, meditate on your calling:

– the soldier

– the athlete

– the farmer.

Anticipate the glory of Christ's return

– the victory

– the crown

– the harvest.

And know that one day too, you will be able to say "I have fought a good fight, I have finished my course, I have kept the faith."

14 December – Hebrews 4:1-16

A two-edged sword

In modern speech a "double-edged sword" is a powerful weapon that "cuts both ways". It's an argument or feature or technology that has a clear benefit and a clear liability. It's something that advances both your own cause and that of your opponent.

But the bible's usage of the term is a little different. God's "two-edged sword" cuts only one way.

> "The word of God is quick, and powerful, and sharper than any twoedged sword, piercing even to the dividing asunder of soul and spirit, and of the joints and marrow, and is a discerner of the thoughts and intents of the heart." (Hebrews 4:12)

God's word is a two-edged sword. And when God wields it, it cuts in only one direction. God's word is not judged by us. God's word judges us. We do not assess it. It assesses us. We do not interpret it. It interprets us. We do not master it. It masters us.

Have you ever encountered the piercing quality of God's word?

Last year I was preparing to help a friend in a court-hearing. We were building our case, establishing our cause, marshalling evidence and feeling more and more justified. And then I read just six words from Proverbs:

> Do not bring hastily to court. (Proverbs 25.8)

It cut to the heart. And it brought to mind other verses about the dangers of pursuing adversarial legal action (e.g. Matthew 5:25-26; 1 Corinthians 6:1-8). God's word came home. It discerned the thoughts and intents of the heart. I could tell you many other "piercing" moments and I'm sure you could too.

So often we come to God's word seeking "discernment" about our future, about our choices. We seek to "discern" correct theology, or just to "discern" a little dose of spiritual inspiration. But all of those motives are about us discerning the word. Or us discerning truths through the word. Do you see the problem?

God's word discerns us. We are in the firing line. We might consider the word to be our object of study. But no, we are objects of the word's study. We are the ones to be scrutinized.

Is that your attitude as you approach the word?

If it's not, perhaps that's because you've forgotten that God's word is "quick" – in other words, it's "alive." When Hebrews speaks of the Word – it has in mind a personal Power working through the Scriptures. Just listen to how the verse continues:

> Neither is there any creature that is not manifest in his sight: but all things are naked and opened unto the eyes of him with whom we have to do. (Hebrews 4:13)

The "Word of God" in view is the Judge of the World. Hebrews is speaking of the eternal Word, the Lord Jesus.

This living Word encounters His people through the Scriptures as they're proclaimed today (Hebrews 13:7). But because the Word is a *Him*, Scripture reading can never be impersonal. To open up the Word is to be opened up *by* the Word, who is Judge of all.

In these verses we learn that it's not simply judgement day that uncovers. Whenever we encounter the Living Word of God we are judged.

"Brilliant" you respond, "Just what I need! More judgement in my life!"

Ah, but the judging word is not the final word. For those who belong to Jesus, judgement could never be the final word. Christ Himself has taken the judgement on the cross. And as our great High Priest, He has brought us sinners through the sword of judgement and into the presence of God our Father.

That's why the verse continues:

> Seeing then that we have a great high priest, that is passed into the heavens, Jesus the Son of God, let us hold fast our profession. For we have not an high priest which cannot be touched with the feeling of our infirmities; but was in all points tempted like as we are, yet without sin. Let us therefore come boldly unto the throne of grace, that we may obtain mercy, and find grace to help in time of need. (Hebrews 4:14-16)

What a roller-coaster! Cut to the heart, then lifted to the throne. This is a true experience of the Word of God. First exposed, then covered by His blood. First pierced, then healed. First judged, then saved. First brought to our knees, then raised through the heavens.

Do we ever impersonalise the Word of God? Do we ever domesticate God's Word? Do we ever get stuck in the judgement and fail to appreciate the salvation?

Remember that God's Word, Jesus, only exposes so He can cover. He only cuts so He can cure. He only brings low, so He can raise up. Let us expose ourselves to His piercing. Then let us come boldly through His priesthood.

15 December – Hebrews 10:1-18

Once and for all

> "Out, damned spot! out, I say!"

Lady Macbeth's line is one of Shakespeare's most famous. In the first act of Macbeth she helps her husband to murder the King. By the end of the play she is in mental torment and eventually takes her own life. In her final scene she is before a doctor and cannot cleanse her conscience.

> "Out, damned spot! out, I say!… who would have thought the old man to have had so much blood in him? …What, will these hands ne'er be clean?…Here's the smell of the blood still; all the perfumes of Arabia will not sweeten this little hand. Oh, oh, oh!"

The Doctor says "What a sigh is there! The heart is sorely charg'd. …This disease is beyond my practice."

Shame and guilt is a disease. And it's a disease beyond the practice of 17thcentury doctors. It's beyond the practice of 21st century doctors. Taking away our guilt and shame is beyond every power on earth, even – and perhaps especially – religion. But in Hebrews 10 we learn about a "once for all" cleansing that contrasts starkly with the old religious ways.

In verses 1-4, we're told that even God's own religion did not cleanse people from sin – it only reminded them of sin. Every day the blood of animals was shed, yet everyone knows that animals can't pay for sin. Every year there was a grand theatrical performance called the Day of Atonement. The High Priest had a starring role and there was a scapegoat. You confessed your sins over the scapegoat and there were sacrifices and at the end it was pronounced that God was "at one" with Israel. But… the next year they did it all over again. They weren't cleansed from their sins, they were only reminded of their sins.

This whole system was a shadow of the coming reality (v1). The real atonement was achieved when Christ came into the world (v5-10).

There is a true and willing Sacrifice who steps forward amidst the bloodshed of the temple and says "Enough! Here I am. I'm the Reality to which these shadows have pointed."

Jesus, our Scapegoat, died the death of every slanderer, every pornographer, every bully, every murderer, swindler, adulterer, terrorist… every sinner. And now

> we are sanctified through the offering of the body of Jesus Christ once for all. (Hebrews 10:10)

That phrase "once for all" is so precious. Understanding it will transport you from the shadow-lands of guilt and perpetual striving to the freedom of Christ's finished work. Therefore in the next paragraph, Hebrews lays out the stark difference between the reality of Christ's sacrifice and the shadow of the old covenant (v11-14).

> The old sacrifices were *continual*, Christ's was once for all
>
> The old sacrifices were *powerless*, Christ's was completely effective.
>
> The old priests *stood* for their constant work, Christ sits having finished the work.

Do you realise the wonder of Christ's finished work? Do you understand that, through Him, you are made holy "once for all"?

The final paragraph will help us (v15-18). Here the writer returns to his favourite passage – Jeremiah chapter 31. He proclaims the glorious truth that our "sins and iniquities God remembers no more."

Imagine debts piling up. You pay off one credit card with another. It snowballs and suddenly you're £90 000 in the red. The debt collectors are after you. You don't answer the phone, you pretend you're not in.

Eventually you get some financial advice. They tell you to phone the credit card company and explain your situation. You pluck up courage and give your details over the phone. Then you begin to make excuses… "Now, about the £90 000, I'll try to pay it back, I just need some time…" The woman on the other end of the phone says "We have no record of any debts in your name." You ask her to double check. She double checks, "We have no record of any debts in your name."

If you've trusted Jesus your Scapegoat, those are God's words to you today.

> Their sins and iniquities will I remember no more. (Hebrews 10:17)

Don't live in the shadows. Don't try to clean yourself up. Remember you've been cleansed through the cross of Christ - once and for all.

16 December – 1 Peter 4:12-5:14

Filthy Lucre

On the surface it's a quaint archaism. But it speaks of a deadly trap. "Filthy lucre" is used four times in the King James Bible and in each case it refers to a grave temptation for gospel ministers (1 Timothy 3:3,8; Titus 1:7; 1 Peter 5:2). Eg:

> Feed the flock of God which is among you, taking the oversight thereof, not by constraint, but willingly; not for **filthy lucre**, but of a ready mind. (1 Peter 5:2)

The KJV follows Tyndale in leaving the Vulgate's *lucrum* untranslated. *Lucrum* is the Latin word from which we get "lucrative". It just means profit. The underlying Greek word is a compound word meaning "unclean gain". So here's what we're being warned against: unclean gain, base profit, filthy lucre.

The repetition of this biblical warning should make us think. But it rarely does. Many times people have joked with me: "What attracted you to the ministry? It can't have been the money!" Everyone has a good laugh. Everyone except the Apostles. They were worried about ministering for the money in the *first* century. What about in the twenty first century when Christianity is big business?

Listen to John Bunyan illustrate the dangers of lucre.

> Then CHRISTIAN and HOPEFUL went till they came at a delicate plain, called Ease, where they went with much content; but that plain was but narrow, so they were quickly got over it. Now at the further side of that plain was a little hill called **Lucre**, and in that hill a silver mine, which some of them that had formerly gone that way, because of the rarity of it, had turned aside to see; but going too near the brink of the pit, the ground being deceitful under them, broke, and they were slain; some also had been maimed there, and could not to their dying day be their own men again.
>
> Then I saw in my dream, that a little off the road, over against the silver mine, stood DEMAS (gentleman-like), to call to passengers to come and see; who said to CHRISTIAN and his fellow, "Ho, turn aside hither, and I will show you a thing."
>
> CHRISTIAN. What thing is so deserving as to turn us out of the way to see it?
>
> DEMAS. Here is a silver mine, and some digging in it for treasure; if you will come, with a little pain you may richly provide for yourselves.
>
> HOPEFUL. Then said HOPEFUL, "Let us go and see."
>
> CHRISTIAN. "Not I," said CHRISTIAN; "I have heard of this place before now and how many have there been slain; and besides, that treasure is a snare to those that seek it, for it hinders them in their pilgrimage." (*Pilgrim's Progress*)

It is indeed a snare and a hindrance. So how can we avoid it?

At heart, we must recapture a vision of the Generous Father. Our God treats nothing as a means to some other end. It is His eternal nature to love the other. First His Son, and then, through His Son and by the Spirit, He loves the world. "God so loved the world He gave" (John 3:16). He is a Fountain of life and love whose glory is to pour Himself out. His activity is not mercenary. He's not in the whole "creation-salvation game" for what He can get out of it. He commits Himself to us for the sake of committing Himself to us. Because this is the kind of God He is. He genuinely loves to give and He gives to love.

Once we've grasped this, we've learnt the secret of life and of ministry. Immanuel Kant wasn't so far off really. Treating people as ends in themselves is absolutely right and good. If even God does it, then it must be the good life. But such living is the fruit of the gospel. It's the good life that comes about with this good God.

So when I'm tempted to minister for "shameful gain" (NIV) or "filthy lucre" I should not be surprised. It's actually a perennial temptation. But look first to the Father, poured out in Jesus. I have all I need in *His* generosity. And look, secondly, to "the flock of God which is among you." They are not means towards further gain. They are my "crown" and "joy" (Philippians 4:1; 2 Thessalonians 2:19). They *are* my reward – a reward far greater than that snare and hindrance: "filthy lucre."

17 December – 1 John 1:1-2:2

This is "the life"

Last year I went strolling along a Mauritian beach with my wife. We bought tropical fruit from a roadside vendor, went for a swim and then lay down on a deckchair sipping a cold beer. I said to Emma, "This is the life."

When have you said that phrase? "This is the life"? You might not like hot holidays. Maybe you'd rather go skiing with friends and then sit down by a roaring fire with a big hot chocolate, extra cream. "This is the life."

Or you go out and celebrate some success at your favourite restaurant with your favourite people. "This is the life" we say.

It's funny how rarely we use that saying isn't it? We live for awfully long stretches of time without saying "this is the life". Apparently most of life isn't "the life". Only very rarely is life *the life*. We have to stop doing everything we've been doing and fly halfway around the world before our life starts to be *the life*.

Can that be right? Is it the case that most of our lives aren't really "the life"? That would be a real shame wouldn't it?

36 hours after I said: "this is the life", we were locked outside our house in the freezing rain, rummaging through our suitcases and concluding that our house-keys were *somewhere on the continent of Australia.* Was this still "the life?" "The life" seemed far away at that point.

I think for most of us "the life" seems out of reach.

But the Apostle John wrote a letter (1 John) in which he spoke very differently about "the life." For John "the life" is not a time or a place. "The life" is a person – a person who was there in the beginning. A person with whom we now have fellowship. Here are the first few verses of the letter:

> "That which was from the beginning, which we have heard, which we have seen with our eyes, which we have looked upon, and our hands have handled, of the Word of life; (For the life was manifested, and we have seen it, and bear witness, and shew unto you that eternal life, which was with the Father, and was manifested unto us;)" (1 John 1.1-2)

This is the life. Not a time or a place. A person. This is the life: Jesus. He was there in the beginning. There with the Father. He came in the middle, to live out "*the life*". And John had seen *the life.* He had walked the dusty roads of Israel with *the life.* And when John saw Jesus he said to Himself "*this* is the life." *Jesus* is the life.

Therefore John wants to tell the whole world about 'the life':

> "That which we have seen and heard declare we unto you, that ye also may have fellowship with us: and truly our fellowship is with the Father, and with his Son Jesus Christ. And these things write we unto you, that your joy may be full." (1 John 1:3-4)

John's greatest joy is to pass on *the life* to us. Therefore we can enjoy *the life*, not just when we're sunbathing by the pool or having drinks with friends, but when we're locked out of the house in the freezing rain, when we lose our jobs and our health and our friends, our family, even our own lives. We can lose everything *in* life and still have *the life.* Because we have Jesus: the Author of Life, the Word of Life, the Meaning of Life.

What do you normally think of as 'the life'?

The life *we* seek is usually self-indulgent. *The life* of Jesus is self-giving. The life we pursue is about sitting back and relaxing. The life of Jesus is an *outgoing* life – from the Father to the disciples and out to the world. Our kind of life is directed towards comfort, ease, distraction, entertainment. Jesus' kind of life is so much better – it's a life of fellowship (with God and His people) and of joy.

"The world", to use a phrase common in *First John*, gives a counterfeit vision of 'the life'. Perhaps today we need to re-orient ourselves to John's vision. As we turn our thoughts to another year, let's not seek counterfeits. Jesus Himself is the life. We need not weary ourselves with other visions that cannot satisfy. We have Jesus, therefore in all of life we have 'the life'.

18 December – Matthew 1:18-25

Thou shalt call his name JESUS: for he shall save his people from their sins

Both Joseph *and* Mary were given strict instructions regarding the *name* of the Christ-child (Matthew 1:21; Luke 1:31). Angels had to come – they moved heaven to earth! – just to tell them *the vital importance of being "Jesus."* Think of all the advice these first-time parents might have received… "You're bearing the Son of God, don't drop Him!" But nothing like that. The one thing they need to know is how to call Him, that is, how to think of Him, speak of Him, identify Him.

And what is His name? Joseph is told:

> "Thou shalt call his name JESUS: for he shall save his people from their sins." (Matthew 1:21)

The name "Jesus" is the same as the name "Joshua". (It's from the same Hebrew word, but translated into Greek and then Anglicized). And just as Joshua led the people out of the wilderness and into the promised land, so Jesus would lead His people out of sin and into God's presence. The name "Joshua" (or "Jesus") means "the LORD is salvation."

So we learn three things from the naming of Jesus:

First, we learn what kind of LORD we worship.

Jesus reveals God Most High. He is the way and the truth and the life, we only come to the Father through Him (John 14:6). So we don't simply learn about Christ's nature when we study His name. His name reveals the depths of the divine life.

Therefore, what does it mean to say that the LORD *is salvation*. It means that His very nature is a saving movement towards us. To know the

LORD is to know Him in His gracious approach to sinners. The heartbeat of God is rescue: the LORD *is* salvation.

And who could deny this when we look to the baby Jesus. From heaven to earth, from a throne to a manger, from King of the angels to man of sorrows. Why? *Only* to save. His infinite riches are poured out in incarnation and crucifixion. He becomes poor, just to make us paupers rich (2 Corinthians 8:9). What is our God like? The LORD is salvation.

Second, we learn what salvation is. You see, the *LORD* is salvation.

Salvation is not a package of spiritual benefits which Jesus bestows. It's not the accumulation of heavenly *things:* forgiveness, a righteous status before God, eternal life, feelings of peace and purpose. Jesus is not like a Prince riding along in his carriage and tossing bread to a pauper. Jesus is far more like the Prince who gets out of his carriage, sets his love on the pauper and pledges himself to marry her. He *Himself* is our redemption.

Salvation is not our receiving of heavenly stuff – it's receiving the LORD Himself. And *in Him*, we receive forgiveness, righteousness, eternal life, etc, etc. What is salvation? The question is *who*? And the answer is: The LORD Jesus!

Third, we learn about ourselves. If the LORD is salvation then *we* must be lost. And that is certainly what our verse describes. The Christ-Child is called JESUS: "for he shall save his people from their sins."

Jesus does not come to save us from loneliness, or lack of purpose, or material poverty. He comes in a very specific salvation – to save us from our sins. Therefore *this* is our greatest need – a remedy for sin.

As Max Lucado has said:

> "If our greatest need had been information,
> God would have sent us an educator.
> If our greatest need had been technology,
> God would have sent us a scientist.
> If our greatest need had been money,
> God would have sent us an economist.
> If our greatest need had been pleasure,
> God would have sent us an entertainer.
> But our greatest need was forgiveness,
> so God sent us a Savior."

Allow Jesus to define your greatest need. It's not your health, your finances, your job, your family, your relationship breakdowns. There is a much bigger problem: your sin.

But now, let Jesus "say unto your soul, 'I am thy salvation.'" (Psalm 35:3). You are delivered from your real problem, and empowered to face all others.

Take a minute and allow Jesus to define for you…

… God

… salvation

… your sense of proportion in life.

19 December – Luke 1:1-38

Hail, thou that art highly favoured, the Lord is with thee: blessed art thou among women

Gabriel says to Mary: "*have gratia plena*!" Or at least, that was Jerome's Latin translation from around 400AD. In English it would read "Hail Mary, full of grace." But that's not a good translation of Luke 1:28.

Jerome's version sounds as though Mary is a repository of some spiritual substance called grace. And if we believed *that* then we might seek deposits of "grace" from the blessed virgin. Yet that is not right.

It *is* right to call her "The Blessed Virgin Mary". After all, Gabriel does:

> "Hail, thou that art highly favoured, the Lord is with thee: blessed art thou among women." (Luke 1:28)

It *is* right to call her "Mary, the mother of God." She does indeed bear the Son who is "Wonderful Counselor, Mighty God, Everlasting Father, Prince of Peace." (Isaiah 9:6).

But it's not right to call *on* her as some storehouse of heavenly blessing. Mary is not full of grace, she is *graced* by God – "highly favoured" as the KJV has it. If we're looking for a Storehouse of divine blessing we should look to the Child who she carries. He is Grace *Himself* – the One in Whom is all heavenly blessing (Ephesians 1:3).

But the reason Christ can offer this grace to the world has everything to do with the *virgin* Mary. You see Mary's virginity is vital to Christ being full of grace for the world.

Mary's virginity is triply underlined in Luke 1. She is twice called a virgin before she is even named (Luke 1:27). And when she's told she is to carry the Christ-child she exclaims: "How shall this be, seeing I know not a man?" (Luke 1:34)

The virgin birth is a non-negotiable of the Christian faith. And this is not simply the assertion of a biblicist. The logic of the gospel demands this supernatural conception.

You see, Mary's child is not the result of human reproduction. *We* did not produce the Messiah. He was a pure gift:

> "Unto us a child is born, unto us a Son is given." (Isaiah 9:6)

And this Gift from on high is something completely new. This child is not the son of men – He is the Son of God! He takes a full and perfect humanity from Mary. But He is the true and eternal Son of God, conceived by the Holy Spirit and born of the virgin Mary (as the creeds say).

This is so important, because this world is *full* of the sons of men. And that, really, is our problem.

Luke chapter 3 ends by running us through a potted history of humanity. From Christ back to Adam, Luke charts our family tree as a succession of men who give rise to more men. But at the top of the tree we find something curious:

> "Enos, which was the son of Seth, which was the son of Adam, which was the son of God." (Luke 3:38)

Everyone else has been described as the son of a man. But in the history of the world there are two exceptions – one is Jesus, the other is Adam. When Adam was brought into existence, his family tree was just him and the Lord God who formed him. He could be described as a son of *God*.

Think of him, standing alone in the garden of Eden: All of humanity was in him. Even Eve herself was *in* Adam and came out of Adam. And between them came the whole world.

Therefore, when Adam fell, he took the human race with him. And ever since, humanity has been born in Adam – born into *his* estrangement and sin.

So the last thing we need is a Messiah who simply belongs to that slow-march towards the grave. What we really need is something new. We need the original Son of God. We need Him to come as the Second Adam, the Man from heaven. We need Him to be born of a virgin to restart the human race in Himself.

And just as we were born into Adam's old humanity, so through Christ we are born again into His new humanity.

As the carol says: "Born to raise the sons of earth, born to give them second birth." (Hark the Herald!)

That's the meaning of Christmas, and it's the virgin birth that guarantees it. So don't Hail Mary as full of grace. But thank God for her. Through her came the Second Adam, who invites the whole world into *His* new humanity. *This* is the fullness of grace that we all need. And it's the fullness of grace which Christmas brings.

20 December – Luke 1:39-56

My soul doth magnify the Lord

How do you feel about musicals? Many people dislike them because '*in real life*, ordinary folk don't burst into song.' Well, hopefully Luke chapter 1 will win over the doubters because here we read, not one, but two examples of spontaneous lyricism!

At the end of the chapter (Luke 1:68-80), Zechariah – the father of John the Baptist – waxes lyrical over the coming of Messiah. But first it's Mary who overflows with praise.

Commonly her words from v46-55 are called 'Mary's song' or 'The Magnificat', since that is the first word of its Latin translation. In many churches it's said or sung on a weekly basis. (In Anglican churches it's most likely to be used at Evening Prayer / Evensong).

Read Luke 1:46-55 and notice two themes – Fulfilment of promise and Reversal of fortunes:

Fulfilment of Promise

Mary's song is very much like Hannah's song (1 Samuel 2:1-10) in which she too was given a miraculous child, she sang of great reversals from the LORD and ended by hoping in Messiah. But Mary's song is not simply a recapitulation of Hannah's – it's the fulfilment of all Old Testament promise. The birth of Christ is "in remembrance of God's mercy." It is what He "spake to our fathers, to Abraham, and to his seed forever." What is the sum and substance of Yahweh's mercy? It is the sending of Christ. What is the essence of the LORD's covenant love to Abraham and the Patriarchs? It is the LORD's enfleshment, born of a virgin.

The Magnificat sounds like it could have been lifted straight from the Psalms. And, in a deep sense, it could have. Both Mary and David were singing of the same mercy, the same covenant love, the same Messiah. The Old Testament is Christian, through and through. And Mary is a Hebrew, through and through. The events of the New Testament are not a departure from the Old Testament narrative – they are its intended destination.

Secondly, let's consider…

Reversal of Fortunes

This song is the battle hymn of a gospel revolution. All our expectations are upended.

> Those who are high are brought low:
>
> The proud are scattered
>
> The mighty are put down
>
> The rich are sent away empty
>
> Meanwhile the meek are lifted up:
>
> The lowly are exalted
>
> The hungry are filled

This is not so much a political manifesto (though it will have implications for all of life). It is, first and foremost, a profound theology of incarnation. Here is what Mary is contemplating: the eternal Christ has emptied Himself. The Word of the Cosmos, has made Himself small. So small in fact that He rests within this penniless teenager. But if *that* is the trajectory of this world's Judge, then all worldly trajectories come under judgement.

While the world attempts to lift itself up, the LORD of all comes down. Therefore the high and mighty find themselves dangerously out of step with their Maker. All who seek their own interests find themselves on a collision course with Mary's child. Jesus redefines majesty as meekness, greatness as service, glory as sacrifice.

For those full of themselves, Christ's coming will turn out to be their judgement. For those who know they have nothing, it will be exaltation for the lowly and feasting for the hungry.

> "Ye know the grace of our Lord Jesus Christ, that, though he was rich, yet for your sakes he became poor, that ye through his poverty might be rich." (2 Corinthians 8:9)

As you meditate on the LORD's humility, how will you consider money, power and status today?

Most importantly, as you think on Christ's self-emptying, won't you sing with Mary: "My soul doth magnify the Lord!"

She wrapped him in swaddling clothes, and laid him in a manger; because there was no room for them in the inn

You didn't choose to be born and neither did I. Only Jesus has ever *chosen* to be born. But if such powers were at our disposal, would we have decided upon the path that Jesus took?

Surely not. Surely we would have opted for powerful parents, fabulous wealth, plush surroundings, an easy life.

And it's all the more justifiable in Jesus' case. After all, He arrives as King. He is taking the throne of His father David (Luke 1:32). Doesn't that demand a certain level of pomp and ceremony? Or at least dignity? Or publicity?

But no, Jesus chose penniless teenagers in an oppressed backwater under the thumb of mighty Rome. He chose to be born in the land of the shadow of death (Isaiah 9:2, 6). He entered our world at its darkest depths. And so His Kingly nature is revealed, not in His high standing but in His lowly stooping.

When the time came, He was not delivered in comfort or safety. In a day when *many* women died in childbirth:

> "[Mary] brought forth her firstborn son, and wrapped him in swaddling clothes, and laid him in a manger; because there was no room for them in the inn." (Luke 2:7)

What John said theologically, Bethlehem's innkeepers said practically:

> "He came unto his own, and his own received him not."
> (John 1:11)

It's horribly ironic. Bethlehem means "House of Bread." Yet when the true Bread of life appears, no-one wants Him.

Nonetheless, Mary puts Him in a feeding trough (i.e. a manger). There He lies as this world's true Food. And thus,

> "Where meek souls will receive Him still,
> The dear Christ enters in."

More on those 'meek souls' tomorrow. But for now, marvel at the stooping Saviour. To see the nature of God, we naturally look to the heavens. Christmas tells us to look down into the manger. *There* is true deity.

As Luther has said:

> "Reason and will would ascend and seek above, but if you would have joy, bend yourself down to this place. There you will find that boy given for you who is your Creator lying in a manger. I will stay with that boy as He sucks, is washed, and dies . . . There is no joy but in this boy. Take Him away and you face the Majesty which terrifies . . . I know of no God but this one in the manger."

22 December – Luke 2:8-20

And there were in the same country shepherds abiding in the field, keeping watch over their flock by night

In science fiction, alien life forms are always showing up from another world. Most often they come to destroy and dominate. In Luke chapter 2, there is a very different kind of alien invasion:

> Read Luke 2:8-20…

These creatures from another world are terrifying. But they do not come to terrify, they come saying "Fear not." They do not wage war. They wage peace.

Their announcement is good tidings of great joy to all people.

Where science fiction aliens say "Take me to your leader" these angels say the opposite: "Here, have *our* Leader – He's wonderful!" What an astonishing invasion.

The King of the angels is born *as* a man and *for* man. For *all* men (v10). And, as if to underline the point, the announcement comes, not to the great and good, but to shepherds who lack even a roof over their heads. Here are the meek souls for whom Christ is given.

Therefore, what is God's attitude towards His world (and therefore what is His attitude towards me)? Well we have it on good authority from the heavenly host: God's heart for His creation is, "Peace, goodwill towards men."

And if we doubt that we ought to make the journey the shepherds make. We ought to go to Bethlehem and see the babe lying in the manger. If we've seen the Judge of mankind wriggling in a feeding trough, how can we ever doubt that God's will towards us is "Peace"? If we've seen the lengths to which Christ the LORD has gone to be God-with-us, how could we ever deny His stunning good will towards men?

If, by faith, we see what the shepherds saw, we too will "make known abroad" the good tidings. We too will praise and glorify God.

The truth *is* "out there." But the truth is not dark and disturbing. It's glad tidings! There *is* life from another world, it is intelligent and very powerful. But this life is *for us.* In incarnation, this life has embraced us in full and wills peace and eternal joy for all mankind. Look to the manger and rejoice. God has moved heaven to earth to bring you peace. He has emptied Himself to the depths of crib and cross to give you His very Self. The deepest of all truths is good news of great joy.

23 December – Luke 2:21-40

Mine eyes have seen thy salvation

> — "Old Testament folks were not particularly *Messianic* in their faith. And even if they were, it was very confused."
>
> – "Expectation for Christ revolved around a conquering Warrior who arrives on a white horse."
>
> – "Believers BC wanted the Messiah to come and defeat the nations oppressing them."

It's common to hear many views like this about the state of Old Testament faith. And, no doubt, many Israelites fell into those caricatures. But they shouldn't have done. And faithful Israelites didn't. Like Simeon.

What did old Simeon do when he laid eyes on the Christ-child? He bore witness to true Hebrew belief:

> "Lord, now lettest thou thy servant depart in peace, according to thy word: For mine eyes have seen thy salvation, Which thou hast prepared before the face of all people; A light to lighten the Gentiles, and the glory of thy people Israel. And Joseph and his mother marvelled at those things which were spoken of him. And Simeon blessed them, and said unto Mary his mother, Behold, this child is set for the fall and rising again of many in Israel; and for a sign which shall be spoken against; (Yea, a sword shall pierce through thy own soul also,) that the thoughts of many hearts may be revealed." (Luke 2:29-35)

As Simeon cradles the baby Jesus, he identifies Him *as* salvation. To see Jesus – even the "little Lord Jesus" – is to see the salvation of the world. And notice that Simeon is not at all nationalistic about this. He does not become excited at the thought of Christ growing up to *crush* the Romans. No, Jesus will be a "light to lighten the Gentiles." He has not come to overthrow the foreign powers but to save them – to save the world.

If there's going to be any over-throwing it will be of Israel itself. There will be a "fall and rising again of many in Israel." There will be a death and resurrection. Through Jesus, the old will be brought to nothing and something new will be raised up.

Simeon sees all this in 8-day-old Jesus. And now he can die happy. In Jesus, all that he's waited for has come to pass. So Simeon, as a representative Old Testament saint, "departs in peace."

The law and the prophets have done their job. They have prepared a people for the coming of Messiah. We can imagine all the righteous of the Old Testament joining in with Simeon's song. The Hebrew saints are accompanying him, jealous of his awesome privilege – to hold the long hoped-for Messiah!

But with the birth of Christ, the time of anticipation ends. Now there is the *establishment* of all that was promised. And Simeon leads the Old Testament chorus line off stage. The time of fulfilment has arrived and so they depart in peace.

As Jesus would say to those who witnessed His ministry:

> "Blessed are your eyes, for they see: and your ears, for they hear. For verily I say unto you, That many prophets and righteous men have desired to see those things which ye see, and have not seen them; and to hear those things which ye hear, and have not heard them." (Matthew 13:16-17)

In a sense we have seen more and in a sense we have seen less than them. We have not held the Christ-child in our arms, but we have read of His glorious death on Calvary. We have not witnessed His miracles personally, but we have been told of His mighty resurrection from the dead. All that was promised has now been accomplished, and so our attitude is encapsulated beautifully by the Apostle Peter:

> "Having not seen [Jesus], ye love [Him] … though now ye see him not, yet believing, ye rejoice with joy unspeakable and full of glory: Receiving the end of your faith, even the salvation of your souls." (1 Peter 1:8-9)

Behold, there came wise men from the east

The wise men and the shepherds tend to get mixed up in our recollections of Christmas. But actually they couldn't be more different. The shepherds were poor Jews. The wise men were rich foreigners. For the shepherds, the birth of Christ was a 'bolt from the blue' as they went about their ordinary business. For the wise men, Christ's birth was a distant certainty that had directed their course for some time. For the shepherds, seeing Christ marks a beginning – they rejoice and spread the word. For the wise men, it marks an end to their long journey. Yet for both the low born and high born, for those with nothing to give and those with everything, for Jew and Gentile, for the expectant and the surprised, Christ's birth proves to be the fulfilment of all their hopes.

In Jesus, Jew and Gentile, rich and poor, learned and common, meet. And with the wise men especially, the whole incident proves that Christ is indeed the Desire of all nations. His birth is not a parochial event for the tribe of Judah. It is truly global. Here is a baby to unite, redeem and rule the world.

> "Now when Jesus was born in Bethlehem of Judaea in the days of Herod the king, behold, there came wise men from the east to Jerusalem, Saying, Where is he that is born King of the Jews? for we have seen his star in the east, and are come to worship him." (Matthew 2:1-2)

The word for 'wise men' in the Greek is *Magi* from which we get 'Magicians'. Traditionally they are called 'three kings', but Matthew doesn't tell us their number, nor whether they rule, (though they are clearly wealthy). The questions we want answered are: Where have they gotten the idea that a baby could be *born* King? How would they know that the King of the *Jews* demands *universal* worship? And what is their view of the created world such that *stars* preach to them the birth of a universal King?

Well the human race can trace itself back, not only to Adam but also to Noah. Humanity has a collective memory, not only of the first Adam and Noah, but also the promise of a second Adam, a second Noah – a Man Who Brings Rest. The Jews prophesied that their coming King would rule the nations (Genesis 49:10) and that the stars proclaimed His coming (Numbers 24:17). Even the nations knew that this Jewish God was Lord of all (Joshua 2:9-11). And when the Israelites went into exile, the

Babylonians, Persians, Medes and Greeks came to hear about this Promised One (see, for instance, the book of Daniel).

It's no surprise that wise men from the east would be eagerly awaiting this cosmic King. Listen to lines from the Roman poet Virgil. Writing around 40BC this Gentile, lost in pagan superstition still speaks of a new age dawning with the birth of a Boy to rule the world:

> Now the last age by Cumae's Sibyl sung
> Has come and gone, and the majestic roll
> Of circling centuries begins anew:
> Justice returns, returns old Saturn's reign,
> With a new breed of men sent down from heaven.
> Only do thou, at the boy's birth in whom
> The iron shall cease, the golden race arise,
> Befriend him, chaste Lucina; 'tis thine own
> Apollo reigns. And in thy consulate,
> This glorious age, O Pollio, shall begin,
> And the months enter on their mighty march.
> Under thy guidance, whatso tracks remain
> Of our old wickedness, once done away,
> Shall free the earth from never-ceasing fear.
> He shall receive the life of gods, and see
> Heroes with gods commingling, and himself
> Be seen of them, and with his father's worth
> Reign o'er a world at peace. For thee, O boy,
> First shall the earth, untilled, pour freely forth
> Her childish gifts...
>
> ...The serpent too shall die..
>
> Begin to greet thy mother with a smile,
> O baby-boy! ten months of weariness
> For thee she bore: O baby-boy, begin!
> For him, on whom his parents have not smiled,
> Gods deem not worthy of their board or bed.

Co-mingled with confusion and darkness, the hope of a baby-boy gripped Gentile as well as Jew. The Son of his heavenly Father would bring a new age, a golden race and even the earth would pour forth its gifts for him. No wonder the Magi brought tribute!

Jesus came not simply as the Jewish Messiah. He was the Desire of all nations and hope of the ages.

Gold and frankincense and myrrh

What do you buy the man who has it all?

Advertisers pose that question this time of year. And usually they answer: some kind of razor. But here's the one occasion where the question is not hyperbole. Jesus really is the Owner and Inheritor of the universe. As Colossians 1 puts it:

> "By [Christ] were all things created, that are in heaven, and that are in earth, visible and invisible, whether they be thrones, or dominions, or principalities, or powers: all things were created by him, and for him: And he is before all things, and by him all things consist." (Colossians 1:16-17)

So what do you give the Man who has it all? The three wise men were faced with that conundrum. And here's what they came up with:

> "And when they were come into the house, they saw the young child with Mary his mother, and fell down, and worshipped him: and when they had opened their treasures, they presented unto him gifts; gold, and frankincense, and myrrh." (Matthew 2:11)

Perhaps through Daniel and the other exiles these wise men from the east had access to the ancient Scriptures. Perhaps they had heard that the cosmic Messiah will receive gold from distant kings. That's certainly what Psalm 72 prophesied:

> "The kings of Tarshish and of the isles shall bring presents: the kings of Sheba and Seba shall offer gifts. Yea, all kings shall fall down before him: all nations shall serve him… to him shall be given of the gold of Sheba:" (Psalm 72: 10,11,15)

Isaiah repeats the thought and adds another appropriate gift:

> "The Gentiles shall come to thy light, and kings to the brightness of thy rising… all they from Sheba shall come: they shall bring gold and incense; and they shall shew forth the praises of the LORD." (Isaiah 60:3,6)

Such gold seems the perfect gift for a lesser king to give to a greater One. And certainly gold *placed on the head* is a sign of kingly rule (Genesis 41:42; Psalm 21:3, Daniel 3:1). As we've seen, Isaiah adds an accompaniment to gold: frankincense. This is because the *universal* King is also a Priest.

Frankincense is almost always used in connection with the temple and priesthood (e.g. Leviticus 2). So the wise men bring a *priestly* as well as *royal* gift to the baby Jesus. He will not only rule man for God. He will mediate man for God.

And how will He do so? This brings us to myrrh. And on one level, myrrh is just another fragrant gift like frankincense. It is paired with frankincense on many occasions – especially when describing the Ideal Bridegroom of Song of Solomon (3:6; 4:6; 4:14). Yet at the end of the Gospels we see a common use for myrrh – embalming corpses (John 19:39). And here is how Jesus will reign; here is how He will offer humanity to God – through His death.

It's a strange gift for a child, embalming fluid! Granted it had other uses but, within the Gospels, myrrh is very much associated with death. And so from the beginning of Jesus' life, He was marked for the cross. As King He would reign from the tree. As Priest He would raise His arms in intercession for the world. In His death He would be established as Royal Reconciler, bringing heaven to earth and earth to heaven.

These are the appropriate gifts for the Man who has everything. Not additions to a needy Christ, but acknowledgements of His Person and work. This Christmas, follow the wise men. Be awed again by your Cosmic King, your Interceding Priest, your Humble Sacrifice. There He lies in the manger for you.

26 December – 1 John 3:1-4:7

Dearly beloved

Imagine two scenarios.

Scenario 1: We are on a ship. It springs a leak and starts to sink. While we're fleeing to the life-rafts, you manage to grab a bag. Unbeknownst to the rest of us, your bag contains a bottle of water and some canned meat – tuna, spam, etc.

We all huddle together in the life-raft, bobbing along the open sea. Eventually we spot an island in the distance. We start paddling towards it and as we get closer we see that the island is incredibly bare. Not a stick of shrubbery, no sign of fresh water, it's basically a big rock in the middle of the ocean. But it's our only hope. So we row towards the island and as we get closer your brother turns to you and says "Boy I'm thirsty." What do you do?

Scenario 2: We're on a ship. Our ship sinks. We flee to the life-rafts. Unbeknownst to everyone you have a bag containing water and canned meat. As we bob along in the open sea we spot an island in the distance. As we paddle towards it, we see that it's lushous, luxurious, full of life. You can see the trees heavy with choice fruits. There's a gushing waterfall in the distance. It's a tropical paradise. As we row towards shore your brother turns to you and says "Boy I'm thirsty." What do you do? Do you give your brother a drink of water?

Surely you are more likely to share the wealth in scenario 2. But why?

Are you a much nicer person in scenario 2? Are you suddenly more moral? What has changed between scenario 1 and scenario 2?

Surely it's this: your vision has changed. You have seen an abundance of life and it's liberated you to be generous. You're still the same bundle of sins and selfishness. But now you've seen something captivating. Now you're celebrating. Now you're assured that things are going to be ok.

In his first letter, the Apostle John makes precisely this argument: Christians are those who have seen the abundance of grace and love flowing from the Father, through the Son. We have seen Jesus and said "that is the life!" Christ has invited us into the "fellowship" He shares with the Father (1 John 1:1-4) and now we share this wealth with others.

The whole letter is summed up in chapter 4, verse 7:

> "Beloved, let us love." (1 John 4:7)

In Greek it's only two words. Beloved, love. *We who are dearly beloved*, may we go and love others.

Because we are not just those who are heading towards a tropical island. We are residents of a kingdom of overflowing life, recipients of a torrent of unending blessing. Children adopted into the ultimate royal Family. Therefore we can afford to crack open our little stashes and be generous with our supplies.

So John would say to us: if we are not loving, *have we really received the love of God?* If we're not overflowing to our brothers and sisters, *has God's love really been poured out to us?* From the fountainhead of our beloved-ness will flow our life of love.

Thus John would have us meditate on that word "beloved."

The Greek word (*agapetoi*) is most often translated "*dearly* beloved" in the King James Bible (e.g. Romans 12:19; 1 Corinthians 10:14; 2 Corinthians 7:1; 12:19; Philippians 4:1). And that phrase is probably best known to us as the opening words of the marriage service.

It's interesting to note that "dearly beloved" occurs seven times in the Book of Common Prayer. On three occasions it refers to the congregation. On four occasions it refers to Christ, "the dearly beloved Son" of the Father.

That's highly significant. The theology of Thomas Cranmer is very biblical here: What the *Son* is singularly, the *Church* is corporately. How the Father feels about His Son is how He now feels about us – clothed in His Son. As Jesus Himself said:

> "The Father himself loveth you, because ye have loved me, and have believed that I came out from God." (John 16:27)

We are dearly beloved. Loved with the very love that predated and produced the universe.

Therefore, as John continues:

> "Beloved, if God so loved us, we ought also to love one another." (1 John 4:11)

There is abundant life overflowing for us. Ultimate reality is not like that barren rock in the ocean, forbidding and sparse. Ultimate reality is paradise. It's the God who is love and who has invited us in. If we've seen anything of His love, won't we reach into our supplies – our time, money, goods, emotional energy – and won't we share what we've got?

Dearly beloved, let us love.

27 December – 1 John 4:7-5:21

God is love

It's universally popular. You can find it cross-stitched on Granny's mantle-piece and emblazoned on a rock star's T-shirt. It tumbles from the lips of bible-thumping fundamentalists and soft-spoken gurus. But what does it mean?

Let's consider four points…

Because God is love, there is relationship, radiance, room and response.

Relationship

1 John 4:8 says "God *is* love." It doesn't say 'God is loving', which would be true. But God *is* love.

This could not be true of a single-personed God. Just imagine an eternity past of utter solitude. If God was an individual, He'd never know anything of love, of sharing, of give and take, back and forth. He is defined by being alone. He is defined by being supreme.

If such a god brings creation into existence it will be the first time he has had to relate to anything. And such a god is definitionally supreme. So how is this god going to relate to its creatures?

This god can only dominate you. This god can only lord it over you. The very being of this god is power and supremacy. And you must be its slave.

But what about our God?

Our God is Father, Son and Holy Spirit (as 1 John 4:9-14 unpacks). Therefore, for everlasting ages past there has been giving, sharing, back and forth, give and take, exalting the other, blessing the other. The early church used to refer to it as a dance (*perichoresis*). And it's a dance like all the best dances when the partners bow to each other and defer to each other.

That has been the Trinity's existence from all eternity. *Our* God enjoys having others alongside. *Our* God lives to bless the other. *Our* God is love.

Radiance

When you read "God is love" in context you realise that "God" refers particularly to the Father. In the next verse we read how "God" sent His Son. So "God is love" tells us particularly of the Father's being. Eternally He has been defined by love because that is who He is – He *is* Father. And fathers beget. Fathers give life. That is the definition of a father. You are not a father unless you have given life. But *the* Father has been eternally life-giving.

Wind back the clock into the depths of eternity and you will always find the Father begetting His Son. (This is what the Nicene Creed means when it says that Jesus is "eternally begotten of the Father." The Father has always been giving life to His Son). There has never been a time when God was not Father – when He was not Life-giver, Lover.

There was a whole eternity when God was not Creator. There was a whole eternity when God was not Lawgiver. Creator and Lawgiver are not fundamental to who God is. Of course we readily imagine that God's prime job description is Maker, Ruler or Judge. But it's not. And Trinity means it can't be. Far more fundamentally God is Love. And He was love long before He was Creator, long before He was Law-giver. Long before He was Judge. His Fatherliness is the most basic thing to say about Him.

Which means that God has always had a radiating quality. The Father has *always been* giving life (begetting), always shining His Light (Hebrews 1:3), always speaking His Word (John 1:1), always loving His Son – and this in the power of the Holy Spirit. God's very nature is an outgoing, radiating nature. He is a Fountain of life and blessing, because "God is love."

Room

All of this means that there is room in God. Perhaps that sounds like an odd phrase, but just listen to how John speaks in verse 16:

> "God is love; and he that dwelleth in love dwelleth in God, and God in him." (1 John 4:16)

What an astonishing thought! "Dwelleth *in God*."

Think of the lonely god for a second. With such a god you might make your way towards him if you slave really hard. But you would always be *outside* Him. Now think of the Trinity. By the Spirit we are grafted *into* the Son and brought to the Father. In other words, by trusting the Son we are brought in on the love that God *is*. We dwelleth in God!

All the other gods keep you at arm's length. In Islam only a few of the righteous will even get to see Allah, on one day and from a great distance. But because the Living God is Trinity we are wrapped up in God. Filled with the Spirit, clothed in the Son, doted on by the Father. 2 Peter 1:4: "We participate in the divine nature."

Response

Finally, there is *response* in God. Think of the dearly beloved Son of God. For all eternity He has responded to His Father – receiving His love, trusting His care, obeying His words, offering His praise – and all by the power of the Holy Spirit. But at Christmas time, this perfect response to the love of God was earthed into our humanity. Here's what John says:

> "God is love. In this was manifested the love of God toward us, because that God sent his only begotten Son into the world, that we might live through him." (1 John 4:8-9)

The Beloved Son takes flesh and lives a fully human life of response to God. He receives, trusts, obeys and praises the Father in our name and on our behalf. And now, says John, *we* live through Him. In other words, we come in on the perfect response of the Son. We live in perfect correspondence to the Father *through* Jesus.

Just as Christ lived our life in our name, now we live His life in *His* name. We not only pray "in Jesus' name" but do all things, whether "in word or deed, in the name of the Lord Jesus, giving thanks to God the Father by him." (Colossians 3:17).

The wonder of "God is love" is immense. But without the truth of Christ's response, "God is love" could only condemn me. "God is love" but I'm full of hate and indifference. "God is love" but my heart is sluggish and cold. Yet God sent the True Responder to His love into the world. And now we live through Him. Hard-hearted, hate-filled sinner though I am, Jesus has saved me. He has propitiated the Father's wrath (v10) and offers the perfect response of gratitude and worship on my behalf.

God is love and now, through Jesus, I dwell in love. Hallelujah!

28 December – Revelation 1:1-20

Alpha and Omega

What is the book of Revelation? Christian psychedelia? Religio-political prognostication? End-of-the-world prophecy?

In chapter 1 we see that it's a *letter* from John based on *visions* of Christ.

> "I, John, who also am your brother, and companion in tribulation, and in the kingdom and patience of Jesus Christ, was in the isle that is called Patmos, for the word of God, and for the testimony of Jesus Christ. I was in the Spirit on the Lord's day, and heard behind me a great voice, as of a trumpet, Saying, **I am Alpha and Omega**, the first and the last: and, What thou seest, write in a book, and send it unto the seven churches which are in Asia." (Revelation 1:9-11)

John is in tribulation as he writes – imprisoned on the island of Patmos due to his Christian witness. Yet tribulation is precisely the point at which we find our deepest fellowship with Jesus. And here John has a vision of Christ – an "apocalypse", (meaning revelation).

Appropriately enough, the very first way in which Jesus describes Himself is: "Alpha and Omega." The phrase comprises the first and last letters of the Greek alphabet and, according to the KJB, it comes four times in Revelation (1:8,11; 21:6; 22:13). You could update the saying to mean something like "I am the A to Z of reality." Let's think about what it means for Jesus to be Alpha and Omega.

Alpha

At key points the Lord Jesus is described as the "First" or the "Beginning." (Isaiah 48:12; Proverbs 8:22; Colossians 1:18). Eternally at the right hand of the Father, Jesus is that primordial *Other* who is Himself the rationale for everything else *other* than God. As the Father's eternal Counterpart, Jesus becomes, in time, the Alpha, the First, the Beginning, the Way out *from* God into a whole universe of others. By the Spirit, the Father's outgoing life radiates in and through Jesus. Therefore Jesus defines and shapes all else. Nothing makes sense without Jesus, "the Alpha."

Omega

Isaiah could not describe the LORD Jesus as "the first" without calling Him "the last" (Isaiah 48:12). Colossians could not call Him "the beginning" without saying He is "the Firstborn", meaning Heir. (Colossians 1:18). And Revelation can never call Him "Alpha" without also calling Him "Omega".

It's not just that all things come from Christ, they are also destined for Him. Redemption is not the salvation of creation towards *another* goal. It is the bringing of all things back to their true Source and Meaning. We are made *by* Christ and headed *for* Christ. In this way, God will be all in all (1 Corinthians 15:28).

What place does Jesus have in your thinking? It seems to me that there are many ways in which we diminish the Person of Christ.

Perhaps we begin our thinking about *God* without Jesus, imagining an essentially christless doctrine of God onto which we add a Jesus-gloss.

Perhaps we begin our reading of the *Bible* without Jesus, imagining an essentially unitarian God in the Old Testament, to which Messiah is later added.

Perhaps we begin our understanding of the *world* without Jesus, imagining an essentially neutral and non-Christian world, to which Christ is an added extra.

Let's reclaim the true meaning of repentance (that is, to change ones mind). I know for myself that I do not think highly enough of Jesus. Yet if we saw Him correctly we would know that we *cannot* think highly enough of Jesus.

Therefore let's determine to repent: to begin and end all our thinking with Jesus: the Alpha and the Omega.

Bottomless Pit

The word in Greek is "Abyss." Jerome's Vulgate left it untranslated. John Wycliffe rendered it "the pit of depnesse". But it's been William Tyndale's turn of phrase that has endured: "bottomless pit"! Rightly, the KJV decided it could not improve on Tyndale. The phrase occurs seven times, all in the book of Revelation (where sevens abound!). Take this representative example:

> They had a king over them, which is the angel of the bottomless pit, whose name in the Hebrew tongue is Abaddon, but in the Greek tongue hath his name Apollyon. (Revelation 9:11)

The sense of the "bottomless pit" (or "abyss") is an unbounded chaos. Infinite emptiness. An immeasurable depth. Limitless nothingness. This place of destruction and corruption is highlighted at the beginning and end of the Bible.

In the opening verses of Scripture we read about a void opened up in the creation of heaven and earth:

In the beginning God created the heaven and the earth. And the earth was without form, and void; and darkness was upon the face of the deep. And the Spirit of God moved upon the face of the waters. (Genesis 1:1-2)

"The deep" is the Abyss. And its presence is felt in the second verse of the Bible!

God, having created a reality beyond Himself, is faced, not with a mere extension of His divine being, but with something distinct from Himself. God is light but here is darkness. God is full but here is an emptiness.

This is not to suggest that such a realm is *evil* – the fall is yet future. But in His good creation, there is something beyond God which needs enlightening and filling full. This is what the work of creation involves. Over the six days God forms and then fills the universe, acting redemptively upon what is, by nature, "without form and void".

God separates light from darkness and sea from dry land. He divides and adjudicates – "Hitherto shalt thou come, but no further" (Job 38:11). God's creative work is all about undoing the abyss. He brings light, fullness and form – bounding the boundless.

Yet somehow there is a sphere that stands against the spreading goodness of God. There is an abyss. And when evil enters the world, the abyss becomes a natural hiding place from the Light of the world.

This realm of evil does not stand on an *alternative* foundation. The only true foundation can be the living God. No, God's enemies have nothing to stand on. Their realm is groundless – a bottomless pit.

Think about this negative reality. The realm of evil is not an equal and opposite kingdom. It is darkness, somehow resisting God's radiant light. It is a boundless emptiness, somehow resisting God's glory filling the earth. It is rebellion without a cause.

Sin and evil have no ultimate foundation, no reasons, no footing. They are madness. Those swallowed by the bottomless pit can only keep falling. Think of the tragedy: it's one kind of death to fall far – it's another to fall forever.

What hope is there in the face of this abyss?

Paul writes to the Romans to tell them that we have no hope against the powers of darkness. None of us can ascend to heaven and none of us can plumb the bottomless pit. But Christ has come down from the heights. And He has risen from the abyss:

> Say not in thine heart, Who shall ascend into heaven? (that is, to bring Christ down from above:) Or, Who shall descend into the deep [the abyss]? (that is, to bring up Christ again from the dead) (Romans 10:6-7)

We don't have to climb up to heaven and we don't have to climb out of the bottomless pit. Christ has done it all. He is the Radiant Light of the Father. He is the Spreading Goodness of God. And He has come to plunder Satan's house (Mark 3:27). He has entered into our darkness and risen to bring us home.

We cannot reason with evil – it's insanity. We cannot climb out of the bottomless pit – there is no footing. But Christ has done it all. We need only trust Him and He'll turn our pit to paradise:

> If thou shalt confess with thy mouth the Lord Jesus, and shalt believe in thine heart that God hath raised him from the dead, thou shalt be saved. (Romans 10:9)

30 December – Revelation 16:12-21; 19:1-21

Armageddon

Armageddon is well known in our culture as the "final battle" for the future of the planet. But the way people imagine this battle differs greatly from the biblical reality.

According to Hollywood, "Armageddon" is a special effects punch-up where the outcome is doubtful right up to the last minute. According to the Bible, "Armageddon" is all build-up and no follow-through. It's a case of "first round, first minute" for the good guys!

Before we consider it, we'll set the scene in the book of Revelation. If you like, you can skip the outline below, but it shows some of my "working" for why I consider "Armageddon" the way that I do…

Outline of Revelation

In Chapter 1: John sees a vision of the risen Christ.

In Chapters 2-3: Christ addresses seven churches.

In Chapters 4-5: As a slain Lamb, the Son approaches the enthroned Father and takes the scroll from His hand – here are the title deeds to creation.

Then we have the largest section of Revelation: from chapter 6 to chapter 20. This shows the unravelling of the scroll. Jesus, the Lamb, unfolds God's history. These chapters show us the history of the world from Christ's first coming until His second.

And so chapters 21-22 show us God's new world – the new heavens and new earth. This is the ultimate "happily ever after".

Most people think of Revelation as a book about the future, yet the great majority of the book tells us about the present. What we see in chapters 6-20 are are 7 action replays of this history from different angles. So we see…

> Chapter 6: The opening of the seven seals.
>
> Chapter 8-11: The blowing of the seven trumpets.
>
> Chapters 12-14: We meet the unholy trinity: the Dragon (Satan), the Beast and the False Prophet (his earthly intermediaries). We also meet the anti-church: Babylon.
>
> Chapters 15-16: The pouring out of the seven bowls of judgement.
>
> Then we see the defeat of the four evil forces…
>
> Chapters 17-18: The destruction of Babylon (the false church)
>
> Chapter 19: The destruction of the Beast and the False prophet.
>
> Chapter 20: The destruction of Satan.

Armageddon

Some may not agree with my outline, but it seems clear to me that these are not seven consecutive scenes of judgement. Here are seven "action replays" of the same reality viewed from different angles.

One of the reasons I take this view is because of "Armageddon". There are three final "punch-ups" narrated in Revelation. They correspond to the defeat of Babylon, the defeat of the Beast and False Prophet and the defeat of Satan. Either God fails to eradicate evil twice but gets it right on the third attempt, or all three descriptions are true descriptions of "the end."

If that's right, then the "Armageddon" passage is one of three angles on the same last battle. See if you can spot the common theme in all three tellings:

> [They were gathered] to the battle of that great day of God Almighty…. And he gathered them together into a place called in the Hebrew tongue Armageddon. And the seventh angel poured out his vial into the air; and there came a great voice out of the temple of heaven, from the throne, saying, It is done. (Revelation 16:14-17)
>
> And I saw the beast, and the kings of the earth, and their armies, gathered together to make war against him that sat on the horse, and against his army. And the beast was taken, and with him the false prophet that wrought miracles before him. (Revelation 19:19-20)
>
> Satan shall go out to deceive the nations which are in the four quarters of the earth, Gog and Magog, to gather them together to battle: the number of whom is as the sand of the sea. And they went up on the breadth of the earth, and compassed the camp of the saints about, and the beloved city: and fire came down from God out of heaven, and devoured them. And the devil that deceived them was cast into the lake of fire and brimstone, where the beast and the false prophet are, and shall be tormented day and night for ever and ever. (Revelation 20:7-10)

Did you notice the common theme? There is a menacing build up followed by a complete non-event of a conclusion. There's stockpiling of weapons, there's amassing of troops, there's sabre-rattling. But the minute God's had enough – it's over. There's a knockout punch before the bell has sounded.

Evil is not an equal and opposite force which gives God a run for His money. As we saw with "the bottomless pit" – darkness is no match for light. Emptiness is no match for fullness.

Do you worry about the future? Does it seem like the darkness will win?

Take heart, the Lamb wins. When push really does come to shove, Armageddon is no contest!

31 December – Revelation 21-22

Alleluia

What makes for a happy ending?

Let me suggest four factors: The good guys win. The bad guys get their just deserts. There's a wedding. And you finish on a song.

There's something immensely uplifting about a story that wraps up with this kind of victory. But the bible claims that history is headed towards just such a conclusion.

In Revelation 19 we see all these elements:

The Good Guys Win

In verse 6 we learn what it is that heaven and earth will sing:

> "**Alleluia**: for the Lord God omnipotent reigneth."

This verse might be familiar to you from Handel's Messiah – it's the most repeated line of the 'Hallelujah Chorus'. (Hallelujah is just another way of spelling Alleluia). It celebrates the day when God will be the only power reigning in the world. No more evil, death, curse, sickness or sin. The Lord God Almighty will rule in unopposed glory.

Perhaps when you thought of "the good guys" you thought of someone else. But the bible insists that the future belongs to the Almighty Father, ruling through His Christ by the power of His Spirit. They are the "good guys". In fact, they are the only "good guys". Everyone else is either with them or against them. But the future belongs to God.

The Bad Guys Get Their Just Deserts

A key part of the future celebrations will be the justice of God's final judgement. We will sing with gusto:

> "true and righteous are his judgments." (verse 2)

And His judgements will burn against the devil and his servants:

> "these [are] cast alive into a lake of fire burning with brimstone." (verse 20)

Brimstone was an old word for sulphur. We have thought previously about "fire and brimstone". We've noted how many people seem to fear "fire and brimstone" *preaching* more than "fire and brimstone" itself. Yet the bible insists there is an eternal judgement for the devil *and for all who follow him.* The bible does not conceal this, it celebrates it.

In the fairytales and the films we cheer when the wicked get their comeuppance. In the same way, Scripture says that when Jesus returns His people will cheer as Satan and his followers are judged.

But notice this: In an ultimate sense, the human race isn't either the good guys or the bad guys. The ultimate division is between God and the devil.

Yet there are those who end up on God's side, and there are those who end up on the devil's side. Therefore the vital issue is this, How do we ensure we're with the good guys?

That's what the next element answers…

The Wedding

> "Let us be glad and rejoice, and give honour to him: for the marriage of the Lamb is come, and his wife hath made herself ready. And to her was granted that she should be arrayed in fine linen, clean and white: for the fine linen is the righteousness of saints." (Revelation 19:7-8)

Have you ever wondered why all happy endings include a wedding? Why are our stories about the guy and the girl finally getting together? The Bible says that all of history is headed towards a wedding. Our future hope is a cosmic marriage feast where we will celebrate the union of Jesus and His people.

In the verses above, Jesus is described as "the Lamb" because He is the great Sacrifice who died for our sins. And His people are called "his wife" because they are united to Him as in a marriage. This is the key to whether we end up with God or not: Are we united to Jesus?

When my wife and I got married we said these vows to each other:

> "All that I am I give to you
> And all that I have I share with you."

This provoked sniggers in the congregation since everyone knew we were broke. Essentially we were pledging to merge our debts!

With Jesus and us, it's very different. We are in debt. Colossally so. Our sins are more than we can ever pay off. But Jesus is rich – royally rich.

And here's what happens when we unite to Him: He takes our debts and we get His riches.

This is *why* Jesus died as our Lamb. He died to absorb all our debts – all our sins – and to pay them off in full. Now He can turn to us and say,

> "All that I am I give to you
> And all that I have I share with you."

All His royal status and connections, all His royal inheritance, all His riches become ours in an instant. That's why Revelation 19 speaks of Christ's people being "arrayed in fine linen, clean and white." None of us deserve to wear white, we are naturally unclean through our sin. But on the ultimate wedding day and in the presence of God, Christ's people will wear dazzling white. Those who say "I will" to Jesus instantly receive His riches, i.e. His righteousness. Jesus takes our filth and gives us His purity. For free and forever.

This is the good news. The Handsome Prince marries the girl in the gutter and instantly she goes from rags to riches.

This is how we can have our own happy ending. It's how we cross over from the "bad guys" to the "good guys". We cannot buy our way into this Family. No amount of good deeds will earn such a future. But anyone who says "I will" to Jesus marries into the ultimate Royal Family. They cross over from rags to riches, from the bad guys to the good guys and from a tragic ending to an eternal inheritance.

Which leaves only one response…

Singing

Four times in this chapter the people cry out in a loud voice, "Alleluia." It's a Hebrew word that means "Praise the LORD." And this is what we are built for – celebration, singing and praise.

When an artist has delivered a spine-tingling performance, when your team lifts the trophy, when the concert of a lifetime concludes on a rousing crescendo, we rise to our feet and pour forth praise. It's ecstatic. And it's where creation is headed. Under God, this world is straining ahead on tip-toes towards the Hallelujah Chorus.

When Jesus returns, His people will shout for joy because on that day the good guys win, the bad guys get their comeuppance and we celebrate the ultimate wedding. We won't just sing. We won't be able to stop ourselves singing.

Spend a moment anticipating this glorious future:

> And he shewed me a pure river of water of life, clear as crystal,

> proceeding out of the throne of God and of the Lamb. In the midst of the street of it, and on either side of the river, was there the tree of life, which bare twelve manner of fruits, and yielded her fruit every month: and the leaves of the tree were for the healing of the nations. And there shall be no more curse: but the throne of God and of the Lamb shall be in it; and his servants shall serve him: And they shall see his face; and his name shall be in their foreheads. And there shall be no night there; and they need no candle, neither light of the sun; for the Lord God giveth them light: and they shall reign for ever and ever. (Revelation 22:1-5)

However your year has ended, and whatever the next year holds, be assured: the people of Jesus are headed for an almighty and eternal Alleluia.

So then, have a very *Happy* New Year!